GOD, MAKE ME

BIG

LaDonna Graber

GOD, MAKE ME

BIG

LaDonna Graber

LaDonna Graber

Psalms 107:2
NIV

PUBLISHING

GOSHEN, INDIANA, USA

DEDICATION

I first honor the Lord Jesus Christ, for without Him there would be no book. From my early childhood days, He has been with me and in me, speaking to my heart, changing me into His image.

This book is dedicated to my husband, Lowell, for his patience with me, steadfast love for me and believing in me. When I wanted to give up, he encouraged me, renewing my strength and determination. He often reminded me that I had a story to tell and that those in a similar situation will listen and have renewed hope and faith. He shared the vision along with me and witnessed my inner healing take place.

Last, but not least, I dedicate this book to each of my siblings—my brother Devon, sister Shirley, and brother Nathan—for sharing our early years together, allowing me to share my story, confirming memories, and being supportive.

CONTENTS

PREFACE

PASSING ON A CURSE OR A BLESSING

Deep within most of us is a story that is buried. We bury it deep in our busyness, covering it up with many things. We don't want to think about it or relive the past. It's better that way. After all, we cannot change what happened, and many times it was not of our doing. In my case, details of my past started coming to the surface forty years after the fact.

Within the last few years, I just knew that God was saying that it was time to deal with it. I am reminded of an old song named "Generations" (2001) by Sara Groves:

Remind me of this with every decision
Generations will reap what I sow
I can pass on a curse or a blessing
To those I will never know

Future generations, our great, great grandchildren, will reap what we sow to some extent. I had successfully kept my past buried all these years and did not want to resurrect it. What was the point? It was painful to relive the details of my childhood and try to make any sense of it. As I started opening up little by little to a few close friends, sharing bits and pieces of my past, I heard continually, "You need to write a book!" or "People need to hear your story."

This book is my story. Some names have been changed to protect individual privacy.

"…Weeping may endure for a night, but joy comes in the morning" (Psalm 30:5).

"You turned my wailing into dancing; you removed my sackcloth and clothed me with joy, that my heart may sing your praises and not be silent. Lord my God, I will praise you forever"
(Psalms 30:11-12 NIV).

ACKNOWLEDGEMENTS

This book was made possible through the love, prayers and support of many special friends. First, I want to thank the Lord for helping with what I thought was impossible for me—writing this book! Father God used some very special vessels to encourage me and guide me on this journey. They each came across my path at exactly the right time, as I needed them.

Lonna Albrecht and Melody Albrecht proofread and made corrections in grammar and punctuation. They always encouraged me and believed it was a story that needed to be shared.

Pam McDonald Eichorn offered words of wisdom, insight and encouragement, pointing me in the right direction.

Pam Wellington, a dear friend, also proofread, made corrections and brought the book alive. She was there walking through it with me, making it flow, and pulling in the details. It felt like I baked the cake, but she put the icing on it!

Dr. Rebecca Wilson was introduced to me by a mutual friend. She offered to proofread my book, edit, add pictures, and work on the format. As an author with a master's degree in English, she was a valuable asset in bringing my book together nicely.

God's timing is always perfect! Harriet Miller, a publisher, graphic designer, and author, stepped into my life according to God's plan and purpose. I marvel that again a mutual friend connected us.

Harriet added her unique design skills to the cover and layout and did some final editing. She was able to pull together each person's contribution for a finished book to the honor and glory of Father God. My Daughter-in-law, Candi Graber, is the photographer who shot our more recent family pictures, as well as my author portrait.

My sincere thanks and appreciation to each contributor for their part in bringing this vision to life and making it a reality.

AUTHOR'S NOTE

During the editing of this book, I became fearful of losing my voice, that my story would no longer sound like me. So I sought the Lord and prayed for wisdom. I heard His assurance within me that, "It's more important that your readers hear My voice than yours!"

That is my hearts desire, that all who read my story will hear Father God's voice speaking to them and that His anointing will rest upon every word.

Devon (age 1) and me (age 2½)

THE EARLY YEARS

During my early years, my parents were not Christians. Life was a constant struggle. The path they chose to follow was very different from the path I longed for, even at a young age. Yet today, I recognize their influence and DNA within me.

While they strongly influenced and marked my life, I still had my own choices and decisions to make for my future. I never felt it was God's perfect will for me to be raised the way I was—in a dysfunctional environment. How much better it would have been to be raised in a Christian home by parents who taught me and trained me in the ways of righteousness. Yet, in spite of it all, God was always faithful. He turned my life around and used me to share with others, helping them find their way out of bondage too.

My beginning years did not mark out my destiny. My identity and who I am is not my past. Scripture describes how I overcame: *"by the blood of the Lamb and the word of their testimony" (Revelation 12:11a).*

Through the pain and suffering of my experiences, God instilled in me much mercy, compassion, and empathy for others. My goal is to give others hope and a purpose, pointing them to the One True Source of hope and deep, lasting peace. Father God has built a servant's heart within me. I take joy in serving others! He built this within my heart, little by little, as I yielded to the gifts and callings He placed within me over the years.

I walk free from condemnation and guilt. *"There is therefore now no condemnation to those who are in Christ Jesus, who do not walk according to the flesh, but according to the Spirit" (Romans 8:1).* My confidence is in Jesus Christ.

FAMILY BACKGROUND

To any outsider, we seemed like a typical family in the 1960's. My father went to work daily and my mother was a housewife. We rented a house, had a dog, and did the same activities most families did.

But my parents were weekend alcoholics. As an adult now, looking back, I marvel at the impact this secret had on my life and how God used it to mold me and shape my life. It was like I learned in reverse. I learned to know what I didn't want to be like from the negative side of life. My parents did not raise a fool. I could see the difference between light and darkness, life and death, at an early age. Just as Deuteronomy 30:19 says, *"This day I call the heavens and the earth as witnesses against you that I have set before you life and death, blessings and curses. Now choose life, so that you and your children may live" (NIV).*

I made the decision at a very young age that my life would be different. Those early years instilled a fear of alcohol in me, because I saw first-hand how it could destroy lives. I swore I would never drink or marry an alcoholic, and I vowed never to live with a man who beat me.

My father was raised in a large family on a farm. He was the oldest son and was taught to work hard. He served in the U.S Army during World War II. His father was an alcoholic, and his mother was a Christian who was involved with the Salvation Army. I never knew my grandmother, but I heard many wonderful stories about what a good mother and godly woman she had been. She had dearly loved her children and grandchildren.

My father was twice married and divorced before meeting my mother. He had three sons and had kept in touch with two of them. We saw them frequently as I grew up. Chet, his oldest son, was in and out of prison after having had a dysfunctional upbringing by his mother and step-father. The younger son, Ron, had moved away from home after high school and had joined the Navy. He later became a Baptist pastor.

Dad's third son, Jim, was adopted by his grandparents on his mother's side. I met him years later as an adult, long after my father had died. He was a police officer at that time. He never knew our father and asked me many questions. He had been told all the negative things about our father by his maternal grandparents, but I was privileged to share some of his good qualities with him.

I remember my father as a very depressed man. He often talked openly about committing suicide by driving his car into a tree. The only reason he said he didn't was because, with his luck, he'd just be crippled and not die. His words tormented me. I always corrected him, reminding him that we loved him and needed him.

As far back as I can recall, he always struggled with alcohol and low self-esteem. When he got really drunk, he would sit and cry because he believed he had disappointed his mother who had taught him about the God she loved and served. He knew that he had made some very poor choices and was now reaping the consequences.

My father was also outgoing and enjoyed people, visiting often with family and friends on the weekends. He liked to socialize and have a good time with his buddies, who were also alcoholics.

My parents

Finances were constantly troublesome. It bothered him that he was unable to pay his bills and provide for his family. He was a welder by trade and painted smoke stacks on the side for extra money. He was a hard worker without real knowledge of how to manage his money, so he seemed to have holes in his pockets. His alcohol habit and poor choices drained his paychecks quickly.

My father was a very jealous man, always watching everything my mother did and how she interacted with other men. She was very attractive and outgoing, laughing, joking around, and having fun. My father was well aware of the fact that men seemed drawn to her. She was

My maternal Grandma Beachy with
my mother's first four children: Alvin,
Marie, Kay, and Harriet

approximately eight years younger than him, and
I think that worried him.

My mother was raised in a large Amish family and
was also a hard worker. She was next to the youngest
in her family. My grandparents were farmers and
professing Christians, eventually leaving the Amish
faith and becoming Mennonite.

By the time my father came into the picture, Mom had been previously married. She had given birth to four children in four years before that marriage ended in divorce. Years later, she told me that her mother had often interfered in her marriage; and looking back, she realized she had listened to her mother far more than to her husband.

As to those first four children, my grandmother and my uncle had made arrangements for them. The two youngest, a boy named Alvin and a girl, Elizabeth Marie, were adopted by a family in Hutchinson, Kansas. For reasons unknown to me, my grandparents decided to raise Harriet and Kay, the two oldest girls, themselves.

I eventually met all four of my half-siblings on my mother's side. As a child I was confused, wondering how we could all have the same mother yet not live together.

In my heart, I believe my mother always regretted allowing her first set of children to be adopted. At the time she had felt the children would be better off without her. She stayed out of their lives so as not to make trouble for them or interfere in their new lives. She felt it was best for all concerned. I remember her crying a number of times to my father, longing for and missing her other children. He would respond, "We can look for them." She always refused.

Years earlier, Mom had rebelled against her conservative upbringing, and she began doing all the things previously forbidden. She started drinking alcohol, smoking, and going to bars. The path she chose was a rough path, full of many ruts and deep

My family: (back) Dad, Mom holding
Shirley, (front) Devon, and me

holes of pain. She seemed to possess a rebellious spirit, insisting upon finding her own way. At one family reunion, her brothers and sisters had told us that she was spoiled and had been their father's special daughter. She denied it.

As an adult now, looking back, I see her much like the prodigal son, leaving home to find her own way. Circumstances can be blamed, but she faced the consequences of her decisions. My mother went through many heartaches and trials, due to her poor choices. We definitely do reap what we sow.

THE BEGINNING

My parents met in a bar in 1951 and eventually began living together, choosing not to marry. I did not know this for a very long time.

I have three siblings: Devon, Shirley, and Nathan. I am the oldest. My parents lived together almost two years before she became pregnant with me.

While growing up, my mother told me about the night I was born. It was getting close to the time of my arrival and she was outside sitting on a fence, watching the fireworks. It was the 4th of July, 1953. She went into labor and my father took her to the hospital. She was prepped for my arrival and the doctor asked if she was going to have a firecracker. She replied, "No, it won't be that soon." I was born two minutes after midnight, July 5th. Little did she know, she had birthed a firecracker after all!

As far back as I can remember, my parents enjoyed drinking and partying on the weekends, most likely to forget their many problems and struggles. Many times, leaving us kids in the car, they went into the local tavern with friends. Children were not allowed inside, so Mom came out to check on us now and then. Sometimes she brought out pop and potato chips. We hated sitting in that car. As children often do when unattended, we would fight and yell and tease each other.

Come Sunday, my parents sent us off to church so they could recover from their weekend hangovers. Local families took us to Sunday school and church. My parents had fought all weekend long, but by the time we returned home from church, they had made up and were on good terms.

I recall coming home on Sundays to the smell of a home-cooked meal, usually fried chicken. How I loved that smell! It meant that Mom and Dad had made up and were getting along, although usually somewhat battered and bruised from the weekend fights, often including black eyes. I always wondered why they couldn't be peaceful like this all the time.

We often found my father watching religious programs on TV. He sat and cried. Mom made fun of him, telling him he was a hypocrite. He once knew the Lord but had walked away from the church to follow his own desires.

The local churches played a big part in my life back then, even providing food and gifts for our family during the holidays. I always saw, even as a child, the vast difference between their manner of living and my family's lifestyle.

One Christmas Eve, my mother took us children aside, explaining there would be no Christmas gifts that year. Although she was hoping to get us a coloring book and crayons, we were not to expect anything. My folks were broke.

She had no more than told us this than a car pulled into our driveway. It was some church folks bringing a carload of food and gifts. My father told

My brother Devon, sister Shirley,
and me playing outside

them pridefully that he would not receive charity and did not want what they brought!

My mother stepped in and said, "Well, I do!" and told them to bring everything in, and she thanked them. Without them, there would have been no Christmas celebration at our home that year.

My mother and Shirley, Me, and Devon at Aunt Vera's

I never forgot their kindness toward us and was forever thankful for them. Years later, as an adult, I went back to that church and thanked them.

I also had several Sunday school teachers who deeply impacted my life. They, too, had no idea what took place behind closed doors in my home. I do credit them for the thirty plus years that I taught children's church and Sunday school years later. I knew what a big difference could be made in a child's life, just as it had in mine.

When I was eight years old, I attended a summer Vacation Bible School at Fish Lake Bible Church. It was there that a child evangelist named Uncle Duane told me about asking Jesus into my heart and living for Him. When he gave the invitation to come forward, my heart raced as I stepped out and made that decision. I was born again and asked Jesus to be my Savior and Lord. I felt so clean and pure inside as the love of God flooded my heart and changed me from the inside out.

Even at that very tender age, I recognized the glaring difference between the church families and mine. And I loved church! It became my haven, a shelter from the chaotic environment at home and a very peaceful place as well.

I believe my salvation experience at the age of eight was a major factor in my life. Even though I lived through and witnessed many traumatic experiences, they could not touch or break my spirit because of God's protection over me.

Father God was now my Refuge and Safe Place. I knew He was The Answer to all our family problems. I often prayed that my parents would change and serve God. And I told them what I learned at Sunday school.

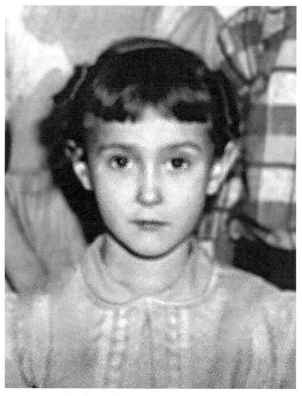

My kindergarten picture

BEHIND CLOSED DOORS

My family lived in a small village. About two blocks away from our home was a creamery that sat by a canal. As children, we were intrigued by this, often asking permission to go and check it out. My mother always told us "no." One winter day, when I was about six years old, Devon, along with Richie and

Sharon, two neighbor children, snuck off with me on an adventure. We headed straight for that canal. It was cold outside and the canal was topped by a layer of ice. We thought it would be a blast to slide around on that ice! We ventured out onto the frozen canal, staying near the edge at first. But pretty soon, I got brave enough to head toward the middle.

Suddenly, a loud cracking sound filled the air. The ice had cracked directly beneath me, instantly plunging my lower body into the icy cold water. My heavy, wool snow pants absorbed water, quickly pulling me down. Miraculously, with my arms still extended out onto the ice, I was able to hang onto the edge. But I could not get out.

Richie, being older, knew exactly what to do. He laid down on the ice and commanded the others to do the same behind him, making a human chain with their bodies. Richie then reached out to me, grabbing my hand. They all pulled as Richie directed, and I was able to crawl out. I was ice cold and my snow pants were so heavy, I could barely walk.

When I got home, my mom at first hugged me tightly, so thankful I had not drowned. And then I was soundly spanked for disobedience. I have never forgotten that experience and still have a healthy fear of ice on water. Without a doubt, God spared my life that day.

While my mother could not give us much materially, she did play with us. In the winter, we'd get all bundled up in warm coats, woolly snow pants, mismatched gloves, stocking hats, and boots. Inside our boots we wore bread bags over our socks to keep our feet dry. She played Duck, Duck, Goose with us, and we ran after each other, laughing. We went sledding with her and had snowball fights. We laid down in the snow and made snow angels. Sometimes she would pull us on our sleds. She made us homemade ice cream out of snow we had collected, cautioning us to make sure there was no yellow on the snow.

Every summer, my folks planted a large vegetable garden, and we canned food for the winter months. During the week, they worked hard and taught each of us to work in the garden and how to pull weeds. During canning season, I helped my mother prepare the vegetables for canning. Because my hands were smaller, I also washed the jars for her. We lived in the country and had a couple of pigs that we butchered for meat. We also had chickens. I was fascinated watching Mom wring their necks and seeing them flopping all over, blood splattering here and there.

My mother's upbringing had taught her how to can and garden and do what she could to make ends meet. Although, I must admit, she did not know how to sew and never made our clothes. She tried, but was not successful. One time I also recall, she cut my hair and made a real mess of it. That was not her talent either.

I realize now that these skills learned at my mother's side have proven to be of great value. All these years later, I still garden and can, and freeze fruits and vegetables for my own family. I did manage to sew many clothes for my children when they were young. Because I had sons, cutting hair was easy, too. A buzz cut at the beginning of each summer was simple and saved us money as well.

My father was a much better cook than Mom, sober or drunk. He enjoyed cooking and his specialty was spaghetti and meatballs. He cooked the sauce down for hours, making it thick and tasty. The smell of that sauce and the Italian seasonings filled our house. We were taught to master rolling the strands of long spaghetti onto our fork with our spoons resting against the fork. He would not allow us to cut the spaghetti. He told us that would ruin it.

He also showed me how to peel potatoes correctly, making the peeling very thin so as not to waste any of the potato. He instructed us to turn the heat down on low, cooking things slowly.

Pancakes were another specialty he made from scratch for our breakfast. Mom's pancakes were always burnt, but his were golden brown. We made sugar water syrup for the pancakes. Another favorite breakfast was fried mush with head cheese or tomato gravy over toast with a little sugar sprinkled on top.

I recall one day pulling weeds in the garden with my mother. It seemed that Mom liked to tease her children until we cried. Then she would say, "Give me a handful of your tears." One day in particular, she teased me, telling me that I had large ears and was homely. I argued with her, but she continued until I was upset and crying.

Hearing the commotion, my father came out the back door and yelled at my mother. He told her to stop it and said she had better never do that again.

Mom, laughing, insisted she was just teasing and that I was a crybaby.

My father called me over and hugged me. He then bent over and looked straight at me saying, "You are beautiful and you look just like me. You be proud of those ears. They are just like mine." I knew my dad loved me. I was, after all, his firstborn daughter. He comforted my broken heart that day, and I carry that cherished memory with me still.

My mother was usually the one who disciplined us. Dad rarely spanked us. Then again, he was not home most of the time, due to work. When Dad did discipline, it was much more severe; his spankings with the belt were harder.

Mom screamed at us a lot and had fits of rage. She had very little patience with us. I'm sure she was stressed out about their lifestyle and lack of money.

Growing up, it was weekends that I dreaded most. Knowing ahead of time what was coming—strife, fighting, turmoil, and much conflict. My folks spent Friday nights and Saturdays drinking. Sunday was the day to sober up and get ready for the week ahead. Occasionally, they had a beer during the week, but my dad always went to work.

I grew up despising alcohol, seeing firsthand what it can do to a family. If I had a chance, sometimes I would hide bottles of beer in the garage, hoping to prevent Dad and Mom from fighting.

The normal weekend routine began after Dad got paid on Friday. He headed to the local tavern where he and his friends gathered. He bought them all drinks. When he came home late, my mother was furious.

The fighting began with yelling and screaming, then ramped up into cursing and fist fights.

Mom didn't care if Dad drank and told him so repeatedly. She wanted him to buy beer at the store and bring it home for both of them. But it wasn't just the beer my father enjoyed; it was the fun with friends, playing pool and shuffle board.

Later, after he had passed out at home, Mom often told me to pick Dad's pockets. I would dig in his pockets to find the money he had left and would give it to her. I have always believed that alcohol is a very slippery slope, having seen too many slide into addiction. It truly does kill, steal, destroy lives and families, and results in poverty.

The cursing and fighting almost always became violent. They threw butcher knives at each other and whatever else was within reach. There was abuse of all sorts. Seeing our parents beat on each other severely traumatized me and my siblings. I firmly believe if Social Services had known, we would have been removed from the home and placed in foster care.

Child Protective Services actually did check on our home once. My mother told us to lie because if we didn't, we'd be taken away from them and would never see them again. This caused me much anguish and turmoil. I did not want to lie, yet what I said would affect my whole family.

Like I always did, I asked God to help me say the truth in such a way that it would not rip our family apart. When the caseworker came and took us children into a separate room to question us,

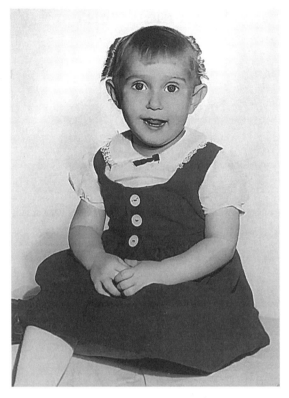

Me in 1956 at age three

I simply told her we were naughty, disobedient children and that, yes, my parents spanked us to teach us right from wrong because they loved us. CPS left and never returned. My prayer was answered, and Devon marveled at how I handled it.

I always loved my parents and from an early age tried to cover up their shortcomings. I never talked about the events that took place in our home, even with my closest friends or teachers.

Although my parents were hard workers, they made poor choices. And we lived poor—in spirit, soul, and body. My parents lived in darkness and under a curse. Many times, I felt like I was the adult and they were the children.

One of my most vivid memories as a little girl was of my mom. I was in her bedroom one day as she was getting dressed. I noticed that she did not wear any underwear. This bewildered me. I asked, "Mommy, why don't you wear underwear?"

She told me, "If I had underwear, you would have none."

The truth struck me hard that day. We did not have enough money for both of us to wear underwear. It was far more important to her that I did because I went to school. I have always remembered that sacrifice she made for me. It meant so much to me and even made me feel loved. Years later, it still brings tears to my eyes.

I also recall how we often walked the couple of miles to a store near the lake to pick up a few grocery items. One day, the cashier talked to Mom, telling her there would be no more credit. My parents had already exceeded the amount allowed.

We walked up and down the aisles anyway, looking at things. Then I saw my mother slip a bar of soap into her pocket. I was shocked. Why was she stealing? I started to say something, but she motioned for me to stay quiet. My heart was racing. I just knew we would be in big trouble if she got caught. After we were outside, I protested and asked her why she would do that. She told me we had no soap, and she would not let us go dirty in spite of the fact that we had no money to pay. I reminded her that we are not supposed to take things we can't pay for. She said, "Sometimes you have to do what you have to do. Do as I tell you, not as I do."

It's a very sad day to remember, to think we had not enough money for even a bar of soap. Honestly, I think the store had extended our credit far beyond what they normally did because of us children.

On the weekends, as soon as the fighting started, I'd cry and run to a closet. I'd drop to my knees and pray, begging God to make them stop before either one got killed. My mother, in fact, wisely kept my father from owning a gun. She was sure that one of them would kill the other with it. They sometimes used beer bottles as weapons. They held onto the neck of the bottle, hitting it on a table until it broke. Then they tried to stab each other with the jagged edge.

It was a miracle they both survived. There were times my mother held me in front of herself, like a shield. She knew my father would not hit me. Other times, I tried to separate them, getting between them in an attempt to stop the fighting. If I was successful, I talked to my father. He sat and cried as he sang hymns. He always said he was sorry. At those times, I reminded him that God loved him and that it didn't have to be this way if he'd only give his life over to Him.

I believe to this day that his spirit was crying out to God, even in his drunken stupor. I begged him to come to church with me, and he would agree at the time. But when Sunday came, he never went.

It didn't help that my mother yelled and screamed during their fights, belittling him. He'd become enraged and threaten to put his fist in her mouth.

Me in 1957 at age four
in one of my favorite dresses.
I liked the chain.

Usually during his drunken rages, my mother herded us to the car for a quick getaway. We ended up driving around until my mother figured he'd had enough time to pass out. Only then would we return home.

One weekend in particular, after the drinking and the fighting got bad, Dad tried a new tactic. Just as Mom was getting the kids into the car, Dad came running out of the house. He opened the hood of the car and began trying to rip the wires off the engine so we couldn't leave. We four children were scrambling into the back seat as fast as we could. My parents were yelling and screaming, cursing, and swinging fists. It was chaos.

Nathan, my youngest brother, was right in front of me. He was not yet three years old and was having trouble getting up into the car. His little legs were too short and the driveway sloped on both sides. To my horror, Nathan slipped and fell, sliding under the car just as Mom slammed the car into reverse to make her getaway. Because I was right behind him, I saw what was happening and reaching down, grabbed his arm, jerking him out from underneath the car.

In that instant, the car rolled back to where he had been lying just seconds before. I quickly pushed Nathan into the car and jumped in behind, yelling at my mother that she had almost run over Nathan. She was preoccupied with getting us moving, but I believe she did ask if he was okay. I was really shaken. My heart was racing as I realized that my baby brother could have died in that brief moment.

But the drama was not yet finished. Dad chased our car, with a pipe in his hand, all the way down the driveway, even running out to the road still hoping to hit the car as we left. It was so scary to us children; we cried and screamed in terror. My dad then ran down the road and hid in the weeds. As we drove by him, he jumped out, trying again to hit the car with the pipe. This happened so many times. I always believed that it was a miracle no one died.

Another awful memory comes to mind. My dad had just gotten his dentures (that welfare had provided). He and my mom had both become intoxicated and were so angry with each other that Dad had removed his new dentures, pitching them at Mom. They hit the cement and broke instead. He went into the house, locking the door so she could not get in. She yelled and screamed and cursed at him. She was so furious, she doubled up her fist and smashed her arm through the plate glass window. There was blood everywhere. She turned to show me; tissue was hanging out of a large, ugly cut on her forearm. The sight made me sick to my stomach. She wrapped a towel around it, but blood still dripped through the towel.

Although still intoxicated, Dad then drove us to the home of my half brother, Chester. They took Mom to the hospital where the massive laceration required several stitches.

Another weekend, they were at it again. This time, Mom knocked Dad down to the floor and jumped on top of him, straddling him somewhat like wrestling on TV. She reached up and grabbed his hair, beating his head repeatedly on the floor, cursing him the whole time. She actually knocked him out; I think she thought she had killed him. Dad's head was injured and blood flowed everywhere. An ambulance was called, and he had to have stitches.

In looking back over those childhood years, it still saddens me to realize that we children spent far too many weekends being traumatized. What I've learned from all these unfortunate incidents is this: When people live and walk in darkness, their thoughts, perspective, and thinking are often not rational.

My first day of school (age 5)

A PEACEFUL FAMILY

It is hard to recall any happy or peaceful moments in my childhood home, where there was always high stress and tension. However, I do have one fond memory from when I was five years old. It was the day I went home with a friend from school and my first time to ride in the big yellow school bus. I was so excited, and I had a wonderful time! It felt peaceful there—so very different from my home. Although I could tell by their surroundings that they were poor too, they appeared to love each other. They asked me to stay for supper, and Mom said it was okay.

When I returned home later, I cried and told my mom, "I want to live like them." My mom did not understand. I said, "They don't fight, yell and scream. They love each other, and it's peaceful there." It seems, even from an early age, I hungered and thirsted for peace and harmony. I wanted to live for God and know Him.

Fifty years later, God used this very incident to minister to my heart. At the time, I was working at the hospital in ICU as an RN. We had gotten a new ward clerk on acute care. Introducing myself, I welcomed Theresa to the unit, telling her how happy we were about her joining us at Three Rivers Health. As I walked back down the hall to get dinner, suddenly I had a knowing within me—a flashback. This was my friend from kindergarten, the buddy I had visited all those years before! I couldn't believe it. How did I know this?

I walked back to her and casually began asking her questions: where she lived, her last name, if she was married, when she graduated from high school, what school she had attended. Just as I suspected, it was all lining up. I then asked the ultimate question: "Who was your kindergarten teacher?" (She thought I was a nut case!) Yes! It was Mrs. Peters! She was that kindergarten buddy from my childhood! She did not remember me or my visit. But I was able to share how deeply her family had impacted my life. I was able to tell her details, even describing her grandparents' home.

She could hardly believe it and asked, "How can you remember all these things and put it together?"

I told her I believed that it was the Spirit of God, living within me, who revealed it to me. I explained how her grandparents, living out Jesus before me, had left a lasting impression. I had longed for such peace. She had no idea of my home situation, of course, and neither did her grandparents. I never told any of my friends about the drama in our home and what took place behind closed doors. She marveled at God's goodness and agreed that her grandparents, whom she lived with, were very godly people.

BLACK HOLE OF SIN

It felt like my father was sucked into a black hole of alcohol and couldn't get out—like quicksand, although it was not really quick but slow, one drink at a time. His addiction suffocated the life out of him and impacted each of us. As for me, I feared that black hole and rejected the temptation to drink. I associated alcohol with pain and suffering.

Alcohol does alter your thinking as well as your perception of right and wrong. An alcoholic can justify almost anything, even molesting his own daughters. Oftentimes, there's a lack of strength or willpower to quit drinking and then maintain sobriety, relapsing time and time again. It's a vicious cycle. I recall my father quitting once, for one month. But then his drinking was triggered again by not being able to pay a bill on time. I was so disappointed and begged him not to return to his old habit. Children raised in alcoholic homes are accustomed to it, and often fall into that hole themselves. It travels from one generation to the next.

In 1963, when I was around ten years old, my half-sister from Illinois, Harriet and her husband, moved in with us. They had no place to live and needed work. My sister was expecting her first child.

One day, her husband asked if I'd like to take a hike in the woods with him. After a long walk, we sat down to rest. He then exposed himself and wanted me to come to him. I told him no and was so afraid that I took off running as fast as I could. He kept yelling at me to come back. I never told anyone because I didn't want to make trouble between him and my sister. Somehow I knew it would hurt her a lot.

A few weeks later, I came home from a friend's house and asked where Shirley was. I was told that Don had taken my little sister for a walk in the woods. Fear gripped my heart as I raced to find them. I knew what may happen; he could not be trusted.

He did try the same thing on Shirley, but she was not as fortunate as I was. She, however, had poured out her heart to my mother, telling her everything. My father was furious when he found out and caused a really big scene. He said many hateful things, belittling Don, and cursing at him. I thought there was going to be a fist fight for sure because they were all so angry. Don and Harriet ended up moving out.

Outside in the yard later that evening, when no one else was around, I said to my father, "Why are you so mad at Don when you do the same thing to us?"

He proceeded to inform me that it was his right and responsibility as our father to teach us girls and no one else's. He insisted that he was preparing us for marriage and that some day our husbands would be glad he had.

I knew in my heart that his explanation was a lie and that he was deceived. I boldly told him so. "You are deceived, and that is a lie!" He did not answer.

And so, even at the early age of nine or ten, I believe the Spirit of God spoke through me that day. *"Out of the mouth of babes and nursing infants you have ordained strength..." (Psalms 8:2).* Again, I felt like the adult. I had confronted him, but I did not tell my mother for many years. I was always afraid they would separate if she knew what he was doing.

Those times that my father took advantage of me and my sister, Shirley, happened when Mom went shopping and he was left alone at home with us. I always begged to go with her, but she wouldn't take me. She said I could stay home with my father. There were many times that he made us lay with him on the sofa or in the bed, putting a blanket over us to hide what he was doing. My father always told me it was our secret and not to tell Momma.

But it was no secret from Father God. It was not hidden; our sin will always find us out and be exposed. *"Nothing in all creation is hidden from God's sight. Everything is uncovered and laid bare before the eyes of Him to whom we must give account"*

(Hebrews 4:13 NIV). When we humble ourselves, repent. and turn from our wicked ways, we are forgiven and set free.

I believe this type of abuse continues to happen today far more than we realize. The internet and social media have made pornography easily accessible, which has also made sexual molestation and abuse more prevalent. We live in a fallen world, but God's grace has increased and abounds abundantly. He always provides a way of escape to set us free from the bondage of sin and death.

It is a known fact that girls who are molested as children are usually sexually active at an early age and are more promiscuous. They are longing to be loved and wanted and to have what we most want—to have a husband who is faithful and desires them. I was molested multiple times by many males that no one would have suspected: male babysitters, friend's brothers, relatives, and my father. This type of thing is still happening to myriads of girls today, more than we would ever care to know about.

I once was invited over to a girlfriend's house to spend the night. In the middle of the night, I was suddenly awakened by someone touching me inappropriately. It was my girlfriend's big brother, a high schooler. I told him to get away from me and to get out of the room or I'd scream. He knew I meant it, and that I would tell on him. He covered my mouth with his hand, saying he would leave the bedroom as long as I agreed not to tattle. I didn't even tell my girlfriend, but I never spent the night there again.

Currently, as a volunteer at the Pregnancy Helpline, I hear the same type of stories from the young girls I see. For some, it has been a stepfather or their mothers' boyfriends coming in and out, or other relatives or neighbors who have molested them. Some people may be quick to point fingers at these girls and condemn, but very few know what they have endured as children in the darkness, behind closed doors. We all are searching for love and for answers to our brokenness.

In a church play in a beautiful
yellow dress made by Aunt Vera
from curtain fabric (age 5)

GOD, MAKE ME BIG

My folks moved several times through the years.
They often could not afford to pay their rent. I recall
many times when the landlord came to collect the
rent. The front door was locked, and we children
were warned to hide under the bed or in a different
room and to be very still and quiet because we were

pretending not to be home. This frequent moving, I realized later, was a huge hindrance to our education. We'd miss lessons being taught at one school and move on to the next, leaving gaps in our education.

When I was eleven, we moved to the Elkhart area, staying with friends of my folks, the Smiths. My mother and father were long-standing friends of Willis and May, who were also alcoholics. Alcoholics tend to stick together, and it was cheaper for two families to live in one house and share expenses. There were now ten children and four adults living in the same house.

My siblings and I interacted with the other six children, playing together and fighting as normal siblings would. Their boys were rough and rowdy, and I was fearful of them. While they intimidated me, they never touched me inappropriately.

In those days as children, we received one glass of milk weekly. Each Saturday, after the women came home with groceries, the kids would all line up in the kitchen and get our glass of milk.

One Saturday evening, my dad and Willis got into a fight in our yard. They were sitting outside and had spent the afternoon drinking and having a discussion which escalated into a disagreement and cursing. They were completely intoxicated. Willis beat on my dad, almost to the point of death it seemed.

The women came outside, calmed them down, and the four of them went back into the house together. It was not long until I heard yelling and cursing once again. Another fight broke out between them, this time inside. I was still outside hiding behind a tree with Willis's son, Felix, whose nickname was Doc.

Although it was now dark outside, Doc and I could clearly see the fist fight through the dining room door, which had been left open. Willis was larger, more muscular and much stronger than my father. The wives stepped in again, trying to separate them. But Willis now had my father on the floor, beating him severely. My dad was no match for him.

Eventually, the women got them stopped and pulled apart. My mother screamed at us four children to get into the car quickly, following our usual routine of a quick getaway. For once, my dad was in the back seat with us kids. The plan this time was to drive around until Willis fell asleep or passed out in a drunken stupor.

My father was gasping for breath and kept begging my mother to take him to the hospital. He was all beat up, bruised, and bleeding. But she refused because he was intoxicated. He begged her several times, and then when she continued to ignore him, turned his attention on me. He was desperate, now begging me to make her take him to the hospital. He thought she would listen to me, but she did not. I cried and pleaded with her to no avail. She told me, "You know he is drunk! I'm not taking him to the hospital now!"

In a panic, I yelled back, "Yes, I know he's drunk, but he can't breathe!"

We continued driving around until sometime after midnight when we returned to the house. She told us to go to bed upstairs and to be quiet about it. "Go to bed" meant that we went to separate rooms—girls in one room and boys in the other. We slept on the floor, wherever we could find a spot to lie down. We'd find a blanket, curl up, and fall sleep. My father spent that night outside sitting at the picnic table, the night air helping him to breathe.

Early the next morning, around five oclock, Mom tiptoed upstairs with a flashlight to awaken me. She wanted me to watch my little brother, Nathan, because she was finally taking my Dad to the hospital. She also informed me that Dad wanted to speak to me, so I should run out quick and talk to him now.

My father was sitting in the passenger seat with the window down, gasping for air. He began by telling me that he was dying, certain he would not return home. I cried and tried to convince him otherwise. He told me to hush and listen because he had important things to share and not much time. I let him talk, although he had to pause several times to catch his breath. I could tell it was very difficult for him to get the words out.

He instructed me to be obedient, help my mother, take care of the other children, and do as my mother said. He promised that she would take care of us. He hugged me and told me he loved us. I clung to him as he kissed me goodbye. My mother then drove away with him, taking him to the hospital.

That was the last time I saw my dad alive. He was 48 years old. He died August 2, 1964. I have always believed that during the night while sitting outside at the picnic table, he had made things right with God, who, in His mercy and grace, is always reaching out to us. He is the God of second chances.

My father knew he was dying. His mother had been a Christian, and I'm sure she had prayed for him. He knew the plan of salvation and had been active in the church years before. Why did he walk away from the church and the teachings of his childhood? I honestly don't know the circumstances. But that night, knowing he had come to the end of the road, I trust that he asked for forgiveness. I hold onto the hope that I will see him again someday. As a parent now myself, I can hardly imagine how he felt, knowing that this was the last time he would see me and instruct me. He knew he had reached the end of his days on earth.

When Willis and May got up later that morning, they asked me where my folks were. When I told them Mom had taken Dad to the hospital, Willis had no recollection of the fight the night before, even asking why there was a need for the hospital.

Sometime later, my mother returned home telling us that Dad was doing better. Since we did not have a telephone, Mom had given the hospital my aunt and uncle's phone number as an emergency contact. Not long after she had gotten home, my uncle's car came racing up our driveway. The hospital had called them saying that my Mother needed to come immediately, Dad had taken a turn for the worse.

Hearing this news, I ran upstairs to the closet, dropped to my knees, and cried out for my father's life. I prayed and begged God to let my daddy live.

My father passed away before my mother even made it back to the hospital.

Before my mother could return home to break the news to us children, a police officer arrived at the house. When he came through the door, all ten of us children gathered around, wide-eyed, to see what would happen next. I held my youngest brother, Nathan, on my hip with Devon and Shirley at my side, clinging to me.

I will never forget the words the officer spoke that day as he announced that he was there to arrest Willis for the murder of my father. That's when it hit me that my father was dead. We were all in a state of shock. No, this could not be true! My mind was whirling with questions. What would happen to us now?

My siblings, crying along with me because they saw that I was upset, then asked, "Sissy, what does this mean?"

I told them, "Our daddy is dead."

We all started to cry and sob hysterically—Willis' six children because their father was being taken away to jail, and us four children because our daddy was gone—dead.

Suddenly realizing that the murdered man was our father, the policeman knelt down on his knees in front of me. With tears in his eyes, he asked me to forgive him for telling me like this. He said he was so very sorry because he had no idea.

I told him, "I forgive you; you had no idea."

I was eleven years old, Devon was nine, Shirley was seven, and Nathan was three. The officer led

Willis to the police car in handcuffs and drove away. Mom arrived home just about the time the policeman was pulling away from our house. She told us to gather up a few things, and we moved to my aunt and uncle's home.

My aunts prepared us for the funeral, pooling their money to buy appropriate clothing for us to wear. We needed to look good on the outside, but on the inside, our hearts were so very broken.

I vividly recall Willis walking into the viewing after all the other people had left. He was in shackles and handcuffs. He stood at the coffin, his head bent low, and his shoulders slumped. And he sobbed pitifully. In a drunken stupor he had killed his best friend. I felt both sorrow and hate for him at the same time. The funeral was a blur to me except for my aunts singing, "I Come to the Garden Alone" (Miles, 1912).

After the funeral, we stayed with one of my aunts for a couple of weeks, but then suddenly we had to move again. Even though my father was now gone, it seemed that life just went on normally, day after day. Didn't anyone care that my dad was dead?

Since we had no money and no place to live, we had no choice but to move back to Willis and May's home—the very place where all the turmoil, trauma, and fighting had occurred. I hated to return there, to face all the memories of that horrible night, where I had witnessed my father's senseless beating that ended in his death. But we had nowhere else to go.

No charges were pressed against Willis. He was freed due to the fact that the cause of my father's death was documented as "pneumonia." Mom told me that Dad had asked her not to press charges. After all, Willis had a family to support, and they had both been drunk. According to Mom, Dad had insisted that he had forgiven Willis.

Just a few weeks later, Willis asked my mother to give him a ride to work because his car wouldn't start that morning. My mother agreed, instructing me to take care of my siblings. She said she would return soon.

By nightfall, she and Willis still had not come back. All four of us children, along with May and her six children, had no idea what had happened. We spent the day wondering where they were and if something terrible had happened. Fear flooded my heart. Now what will happen to my brothers and sister and me? I prayed over and over, "Father God, make me *big* so I can take care of them."

After much investigation and searching, we discovered that Willis and my mom were having an affair. They were found in a hotel room together. My siblings and I were taken to my aunt's house until it was decided what to do with us. I continually prayed, "Father God, make me *big* so I can take care of my brothers and sister."

My childhood had vanished, and I was feeling responsible for my siblings. My father was dead, and my mother was bringing shame and embarrassment to our family. At eleven years old, I knew that what had taken place was wrong. I had many questions. I felt broken and crushed. What would happen to us now?

HEALING THE BROKEN-HEARTED

Years later, I told someone about my prayer of asking God to make me big, but I concluded that He hadn't. In that moment the Spirit of God corrected me and spoke to my heart. I was reminded of the prayer of Jabez: *"Jabez cried out to the God of Israel, 'Oh that you would bless me and enlarge my territory! Let your hand be with me, and keep me from harm so that I will be free from pain.' And God granted his request"* (1 Chronicles 4:10 NIV).

I realized right then that God had indeed answered my childhood prayer by enlarging my spirit within me far beyond my youth and giving me Divine wisdom and understanding.

God proved Himself faithful to be with me always, even in those dark days. As a child, there were many things I did not understand. But I see now, in looking back, that God alone knew what I had been through and how I felt. Even though I had a broken heart, I learned to lean on Him and trust Him with every detail.

Thank God, *"The spirit of the Lord is upon me. Because He has anointed me to preach the gospel to the poor: To proclaim liberty to the captives and recovery of sight to the blind, to set at liberty those who are oppressed: to proclaim the acceptable year of the Lord"* (Luke 4:18 NIV).

When my mother was found in the motel room with Willis, my aunts informed her that if she did not immediately return for her children, we would be put in an orphanage. Crouching outside below a kitchen window, I heard my aunts' conversation as they discussed what to do with us. One aunt declared, "I don't want those snotty-nose brats around here." I felt rejected by my entire family. First, my father left us, dying in a way that made no sense, then my mother ran off, seemingly with no concern for her children. And now my aunts were discussing us as though we were nothing to them. I was very angry, bitter, and hurt. I had been through so much already and was old enough to know that most everything that had happened was wrong. Many years later, I confronted that aunt and told her that I had heard what she said. She denied making that statement, insisting that she had been talking about the neighbor kids, not us. Either way, I forgave her.

When my mother returned for us, Willis was with her. My heart sank. So it was true; they were having an affair. Disappointment was now added to my anger.

At first I refused to go with her or to have anything to do with her. Bitter and ashamed, I told her I'd rather go to an orphanage than live with her. My aunt stepped in, instructing Mom to take me to the bedroom and talk to me alone. When we got into the bedroom, she closed the door. She told me that I had to come with her. From the abundance of my brokenness, pain, and bitterness, I poured out my heart. I called my mother every filthy, foul name I could remember—all the filthy words I had heard repeatedly as a child.

"You're nothing but a whore!" I screamed.

She fired back, "Well, aren't you something! It's only been a few short weeks since you made your father a promise—his dying request. Look how quickly you forgot your promise to your dad" (to be obedient and do as she says).

I stopped, realizing what she said was true. But my anger still burned.

"Very well," I said, "I will go with you. And now I'm making you a promise! You will regret the day I was born, and I will make your life hell on earth!"

I expected to be slapped for mouthing off to her; instead, I think she was stunned. To smooth things over, she promised to take us to the Centreville Fair if we all would come with her peacefully. But that never happened. She had lied to me. Again.

My father died on August 2. It was now mid-September. So much had happened in one short month. I thought the worst thing in the world happened when my dad died, but the circumstances seemed to get worse daily.

Mother then took us to the home of my half-brother, Chester. He lived with his wife and her three children—Paula Sue, Wally, and Kevin—and their daughter together—LuAnn. Willis came along with us. Years later, I confronted Chet about him allowing them to live there together with us.

Chet said, "I wanted to take care of you kids. I knew your mom would not let me have you unless they could stay here, too." He reminded me that Mom had already given up her first four children, and he didn't want her to give up four more.

That month with Chet was very difficult as well. We changed schools again, for the second time that fall. But most of all, it was extremely painful to see Willis and my mother together in bed, his arms wrapped around her. I despised and hated him and had no respect for my mother.

After about a month, Willis deserted her, going back to his wife and six children. He lied to my mother, saying that he needed to go home to get some clothes. She rode along with him, but when they arrived at his house, he told her to wait in the car. He never came back out, but his wife sure did! May gave my mother a tongue lashing, telling her exactly what she thought of her. She screamed at her, demanding she leave and never come back! Returning to Chet's house, my mother was weeping and broken, fearful, rejected, and ashamed.

I told her, "Pull yourself up by your boot straps, and get on with your life! He is not your husband and you don't need him. Let's get out of here!"

Once again, I felt that between the two of us, I was the adult.

THE PAST COMES CALLING

Years later, as a nurse at the local hospital, I was asked to take care of a patient named Felix. Since that was such an usual name, I immediately wondered if this could be the same Felix I had known all those years ago. Could it be the young boy who had stood with me behind the tree watching our fathers fight? Could this possibly be the same person?"

When I went into his room, I looked at his name band and then greeted him by his nickname. "Hello Doc."

He was startled. "How do you know my nickname?"

I asked him if he recognized me. He said I looked familiar, and continued studying my face. From the change in his expression, I could tell when it dawned on him who I was.

I asked, "Do you remember that night?"

He solemnly replied, "How could I ever forget?"

I inquired about his family. He told me that some of his siblings had died young and that his dad had died a long, agonizing death from cancer. His family had gone through many struggles and heartaches. Furthermore, he told me his dad was never the same after my father's death; he had become very angry and bitter at the world.

I told him, "Your dad could not forgive himself for what he had done, and so he was hateful to all of you."

It struck me that here was another family that had suffered and was destroyed by alcohol. I was thankful once again that my intensely painful experience with alcohol had convinced me not to drink. But I know it's *"not what goes into a man that defiles a man, but what comes out of the mouth. This defiles a man" (Matthew 15:11).* Out of the abundance of our hearts, our character and integrity are revealed, as well as who we serve.

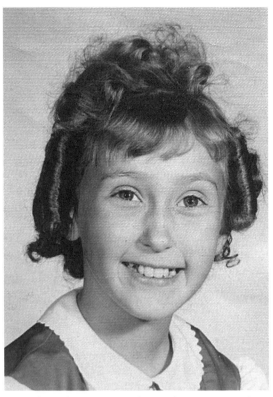

School picture (grade 3, age 7)

GOD IS ALWAYS WORKING

Once I started writing this book, I came to a place where I felt like I was in a holding pattern. I knew I was supposed to wait; and I am so glad I did. The only thing worse than waiting on God... is wishing you had.

In the meantime, I had lost all contact with Doc and the rest of the Smith family. With the help of the internet, I found a man named Daniel Smith. I messaged him, explaining who I was. I asked if he was related to Willis and May. I had guessed that he must be since his online picture looked just like Willis as I remembered him from my childhood. I also figured that Daniel was a grandson; I was right.

We shared memories back and forth. Daniel was Willis' grandson and the son of Louie, Willis' oldest son. Daniel did not remember me, but his mother did. He did remember visiting my family and that his grandpa liked to hang out with my dad. He also recalled that they came frequently to go fishing. I asked Daniel, "So what do you do? What is your life's work?"

I was shocked when he said he was a pastor! He admitted that it was nothing short of a miracle.

At the age of 31, he had come to the end of himself and intended to end his life. But God called out to him, telling him not to do it. He was saved—born again—and called to preach in 1991. God has been in control, he told me, ever since. He confessed that he had repeated all the bad, evil, sinful things the Smith family had always done, but God had another plan. *"For I know the thoughts that I think toward you, says the Lord, thoughts of peace and not of evil, to give you a future and a hope" (Jeremiah 29:11).*

Daniel also shared that Willis and Louie had each received Christ on their death beds. Others, including Felix, were all born again and now served God.

I was so excited! I called my siblings. We rejoiced that God had touched the Smith family's hearts.

Chester (Chet) and Ron, Dad's sons
and my half brothers

This knowledge also brought healing and closure to my heart regarding that part of my past.

After Willis left Mom, we remained with my oldest step-brother, Chet. I assumed things would get better now that Willis wasn't around, but they didn't.

Mom, at 40 years of age, was still very attractive and dated several men off and on. It was like bees to honey. She was gone most of the time, and we children all missed her greatly. Her absence only added to the feelings of loss. While I was hopeful things would change, Mom was on a mission to find a father for us. Most of the men she dated wanted her but not the responsibility of four children. She would not give us up. This caused me to believe that my mother truly did love us after all.

During the time Mom was seeking a husband to father her four children, she met Warren Soule at a bar. This man would become my stepdad. He wanted to marry her and agreed to take on four stepchildren. He also had had a troubled life and had given up four sons. At this time in my life, I would not have accepted even the godliest man on earth. I still loved and longed for my dad and was hurting deeply at the circumstances life had dealt me. I had many wounds in my soul, my mind, my heart, and my emotions.

I always knew that God was with me and loved me, and I did not forget my commitment to Him. However, I could not understand why my life was so tragic. I just couldn't come to terms with it all. It seemed my world was falling apart. I desired to know God in a more intimate way, but I needed teaching, instruction, and godly examples. I also needed to renew the Word of God in my mind. I needed people who could show me a godly example and come alongside me, mentoring me.

Little did I know, God had a plan; He had not forsaken me. I knew in my heart that He was my only hope for a good life marked by His peace. I vowed I would not live the rest of my life as I had thus far.

While I missed my father terribly, I also knew it was probably better for my sister and me that he was gone because of his habitual molestation. Even though I still loved him, I always thought of him as a weak and broken man.

I don't know if my father grew up with abuse. Neither do I know the heartaches he must have carried. It's by God's grace that I have mercy and forgiveness towards him.

AFTER 55 YEARS, RECONNECTED AND REUNITED

A strange thing happened years later when I was an RN for Homecare and Hospice. I was asked to fill in by calling on a few patients. While looking over the paperwork, I noted the name Paula. The last name did not mean anything to me, but the thought came, "I wonder if this could be the Paula who had lived at Chester's house those many years ago?"

I phoned before heading out on my calls. Although it had been 55 years since I'd last seen Paula, I instantly recognized her voice when she answered. I stated my name, saying that I was calling to set up an appointment for a home visit.

She asked, "What is your name again?"

I said, "LaDonna."

She said, "Is this my LaDonna?"

I answered, "Is this my Paula?"

We both started laughing and could hardly believe it! After many decades, we were reconnected.

We got together and spent two hours sharing our stories. How differently our lives had turned out from the way we were raised. She, too, was now a Christian. I found out that her brother, Wally, was dying of cancer. I had an opportunity to go see him and pray with him, giving me further closure from past hurts.

The very next week, I was once again seeing patients. This time, I was sent to the very house we had lived in with Chester. Here was yet another tangible memory, reconnecting me with Paula.

I just marveled at how God works. While thinking, "God, what are you up to?" I told the patient, "I have a story for you."

These people, I discovered that day, had bought the house shortly after we moved out. I thought, "Father God, You are awesome, and You've got my number." *"The steps of a good man are ordered by the Lord, and He delights in his way" (Psalm 37:23).*

MY FATHER'S INFLUENCE ON ME

I was about fifty years old when I decided to seek a Christian counselor, hoping to sort out my heart issues. To my surprise, the counselor told me that it was not normal for me to love my dad because of all the abuse I had endured from him. My younger sister was apparently more normal, because she was still very bitter at the time. Eventually, however, she did forgive our father.

My counselor's first assignment for me was to go home and ask God to reveal why I loved my father and held no bitterness toward him. One morning soon after, God revealed the answer to me. I had been born again at eight years old and, by the Holy Spirit, God's love had been awakened in my heart

Dad with Chester,
his oldest child and my half brother

from that very moment. *"And above all things have fervent love for one another, 'for love will cover a multitude of sins'" (1 Peter 4:8).* The light came on. I had covered my father's sin with God's love. My counselor marveled at my answer, believing it to be true. God's love had been my saving grace, allowing me to show mercy and compassion.

In those short eleven years I knew him, my father taught me things that would empower me later in life. For one, he was not a racially prejudiced person. He told me that the color of a person's skin did not matter because that's only on the outside. Our blood on the inside was the same color. What really matters, he told me, is what's inside a person's heart.

He was also a hard worker, refusing to take handouts or charity. When we were on welfare, he worked at cleaning up the roadways. My father invited people into our home who were broke and needed a place to live. My mother would get upset at him for bringing these people home with him from the bar, saying, "We don't even have enough for our children, so how can we help them?"

He would calmly answer, "Ma, we have more than they do. How can we not help them?"

He found them jobs, and drove them back and forth to work. If they refused to work or were lazy, he kicked them out. He believed if you didn't work, you didn't eat. God used his example to instill in me a deep compassion for others that were in need of a helping hand.

Years later, I opened our home to those in need. Up to now, we've taken in several individuals for varying lengths of time, depending upon the situation. Some were relatives and some were not. We housed foster children and teenagers when I was a volunteer probation officer for troubled teens. We also provided housing for a family of five until they got back on their feet, assisting them in getting work. We charged no money when people came to live with us. Other people often asked, "Doesn't that bother you, taking in needy people?"

I simply told them, "That's how I was raised; we grew up helping others."

For me, it was just a normal way of life; however, it was an adjustment for my husband and sons. We had some wonderful experiences helping others. I took to heart the scripture where Jesus said, *"Inasmuch as you did it to one of the least of these my brethren, you did it to me" (Matthew 25:40b).* I also told my husband, *"For everyone to whom much is given, from him much will be required" (Luke 12:48b).* I believe that we are blessed to be a blessing to others.

Because I was my dad's firstborn daughter, having had only sons before me, I always knew that my dad loved me and that I was special to him. He had loved and respected his mother and remembered her as a Godly woman. I know he felt like he had disappointed her. Although she had taught and trained him in the ways of God, he had chosen the path of his father, that of an alcoholic. Many years after my dad died, I had a dream about him.

Dad was 'beamed' into our log home and was standing in our living room, looking up at the 24-foot-high ceilings. My husband, Lowell, and I were standing behind the kitchen counter, several feet away, watching. Lowell asked, "Who is that?"

I told him, "That's my father; come with me and I'll introduce you."

My dad looked just as I remembered. I walked over to him and introduced him to Lowell. "This is my husband of 42 years."

Lowell and I in our kitchen

He just looked at me, bewildered, like he could not believe that his little girl was all grown up and married. He never uttered a word, but somehow I knew his thoughts. He wondered if I was happy and if Lowell was good to me. I could tell he was concerned.

I told him, "Yes, Dad, he is a good man." Hearing not with my ears but with my heart, he told me how he was so sorry for everything. He began weeping. Wrapping his arms around me, he put his head on my shoulder and continued to sob. Love flowed from him. He knew he had missed so much.

I woke up sobbing myself, knowing I had been given a gift from God in that special "visitation."

I cried for days afterwards, thinking of the many things I wished I had told him. The whole experience was so real.

I called my siblings and told each of them about the dream. For me it was a final closure to my dad's death and all that had happened. He was sorry, and I was loved. That was the first and only time I dreamt about my father.

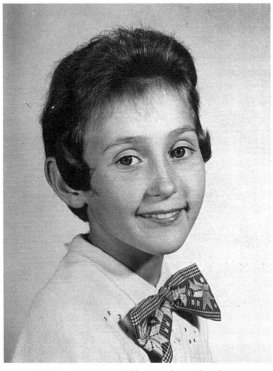

1962 Centreville school photo
(grade 4, age 9)

LIFE WITH A STEPFATHER

Life with my stepfather, Warren, was more stable. We had a place to live, and he never attempted to molest me or my sister. Warren was insistent that we call him Dad, out of respect. I rebelled against this and often would not, even telling him that he was not my father.

Family photo: (front) Warren, my mother holding Jacob (my half brother); (back) Devon, Shirley, me, Nathan

He wanted to adopt us, giving us his last name, but I refused. I wanted to carry my dad's name until the day I married because it was the one thing my father had left me.

That upset Warren. He told me I didn't really have Dad's name because I was nothing but a bastard. His words felt like a sharp knife thrust into my heart. I was devastated, refusing at first to believe it. I asked my mother if his accusation was true; and she admitted it was.

That was the moment I found out that my parents had never married. It felt like my whole life, up to this point, had been a lie. Not only was my father dead, but I really did not have his name. Mom reassured me, though, that Daddy was my real father.

Several years later, while volunteering at the Pregnancy Helpline doing ultrasounds, Father God brought that incident with Warren back to my remembrance.

An 18-year-old came in for an ultrasound, and I asked if this was her first pregnancy. She told me it was her third. She already had two sons in foster care because her parental rights had been terminated. I asked if the young man in the waiting room was the father of the baby she was carrying. She told me no, reassuring me that he didn't care that the child wasn't his.

My thought was, "Will this child have a chance? Will his life be any different than the rest of the children born into similar circumstances?"

I was up early the next morning, praying, and this girl came to mind. I was still wondering if things would be different for this child. The Lord reminded me about my own mother giving up her first four children for adoption, that I was her fifth child, and that she had never married my father. "Is your life different? Have I made a difference in your life? You're my child and you have chosen a different path to follow."

I wept, realizing anew that God loves us all and gives us the freedom to choose blessings or curses. My life is different because of Him. Armed with a better attitude toward this young woman and her baby, I covered them with prayer.

NEW PARENT/NEW RULES

Warren was strict and controlling, not at all like my father. He had a lot of rules and regulations. It wasn't long before he and my mother were not getting along either, and there was fighting in our home once again.

Together they had a son, Jacob. Warren was partial toward Jacob, favoring his own flesh and blood over the rest of us. But I figured that was to be expected. He told the rest of us repeatedly, "You will never amount to nothing."

Looking back, I see that I needed his discipline and stability in my life. Warren tried to be a good father to us, but he really didn't know how, never having dealt with his own issues from the past. Romans 8:28 says: *"And we know that all things work together for good to those who love God, to those who are the called according to His purpose."*

And so it was that I lived through more painful years, but I knew in my heart that God loved me and had a plan for my life. My circumstances were not of my doing, and I was determined I would not live like my parents, but I would have a far better life. God says in His Word, *"This day I call the heavens and the earth as witnesses against you that I have set before you life and death, blessings and curses. Now choose life, so that you and your children may live" (Deuteronomy 30:19 NIV).* It was an open book test. I made my choice to live for God, and He lived in me, leading and guiding me.

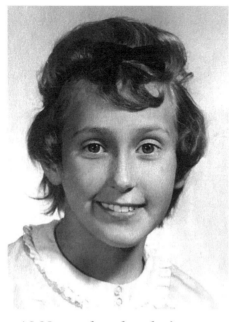

1963 gradeschool picture
(grade 5, age 10)

While living at Warren's, I went back to church, participated in the youth group, and made new friends. I found part-time jobs in the neighborhood: babysitting, cleaning houses, pulling weeds, and ironing. I was able to buy school clothes for myself with my earnings.

Our next door neighbor, Mrs. Kadell, hired me to clean her house a couple days a week. She had about twenty cats inside, so there was always a lot to clean. She kept a record of my earnings for me at her house. She knew I wanted to buy school clothes with the money, and she was afraid my parents would spend it. In August, before school started, she would tally the amount I had made that summer.

Warren and Me at my 25th wedding
anniversary celebration

From her mail-order catalog I would pick the clothes I wanted, and she would order them for me.

My mother and I did not always see eye to eye, but she would often talk to me like I was her friend, rather than her child. Before marrying Warren, she had even asked me if she should marry him.

My answer was, "If you don't know, and you have to ask an eleven-year-old girl who has never even dated or had a boyfriend, then probably not!" Again, feeling like the adult, I told her I really didn't care if she did marry Warren because as soon as I could, I was moving out of there to be on my own. She married Warren shortly afterward, on January 1, 1965, just five short months after my father's death. I was never really sure if my mom loved Warren or if she just needed someone to help raise her children.

In spite of their conflicts, Warren and Mom managed to stay together. They liked to go to bars, drinking and partying, on the weekends, and they also enjoyed square dancing. It seemed like the old saying was true: Some things never change. We did have family time quite often, playing baseball and roasting hotdogs.

Warren believed if he could win me over, he could win my younger siblings as well. But, knowing the strong influence I had over my younger siblings, I would tell them, "He is not our dad. We had a dad, and it's not Warren."

The following summer before school, Warren offered to take me shopping for school clothes. He said he would take one of us every week until we all had new clothes. I was hesitant to be alone with him, not trusting any men in those days, but I went. I picked out some new dresses I liked, and

Nathan, Shirley, Me, and Devon

our time together was uneventful. The next week, I asked which of my younger siblings would be getting their school clothes next. I was told there was no money left, and that they would have to get by with their old clothes.

Feeling deceived, I declared, "If that's the case, take mine back to the store. I will not wear them. If my brothers and sister don't get new clothes, then neither do I."

I felt bad for my siblings; it was not fair; and the clothes were returned. Looking back, I realize that God had already given me a strong knowledge of right and wrong. I had a lot yet to learn about the love of God, but I already knew something about justice.

NEAR DROWNING

Warren's boys, Bob and Bill, would occasionally come over. They lived with their grandparents. His other two sons had been adopted by his brother.

One day, my brother Devon, Bob, and I went swimming at the Langley Covered Bridge. We decided to swim across the wide river to the other side. Being boy scouts, Devon and Bob were excellent swimmers. I could swim, but I tired more easily, not having the strength they did. We got halfway across the river when I realized I was not going to make it. I started to panic. Bob swam to me and instructed me to roll over onto my back and relax. He then pulled me to shore with a lifesaving technique.

I have never forgotten his heroic act and have always been grateful to him for saving me from drowning that day. Once again, I recognized that God's hand was upon me. He was not done with me.

Bob eventually came to live with us. One morning before school, my mom was in a really bad mood, screaming at Bob and belittling him as she often did. Bob just ignored her, but I didn't. I came to his defense. "Why don't you get off his back and leave him alone!" It was in that moment that I learned what disrespecting my mother would bring. She backhanded me so hard, I fell to the floor.

My mother said, "Don't you ever talk to me like that again!"

I got up, grabbed my school books, and walked out crying. But in my heart, I was glad that I had stood up for Bob.

He told me later, "Thanks, but you didn't have to do that."

I told him, "It's not right that she treats you so bad."

MAKING CHOICES

By this time I was in high school. My family had moved to the town of Centreville, where I walked to school. I liked a boy from school named Rodney and suspected he had a crush on me as well. He would come to my locker and talk to me and then carry my books as we walked to class. After a few weeks, he asked me to go to a Friday night football game, and I was thrilled.

While walking home from school one afternoon, I noticed a car parked up ahead along the roadside. I could hear loud music along with laughter and yelling coming from inside the car. As I passed by, Rodney suddenly spotted me and got out of the car. I could tell they had been drinking and carrying on. He walked over to me, smiling.

I said, "Oh, I'm glad I saw you. I won't be able to go to the football game. Something has come up."

"What do you mean? We had a date."

"Not anymore," I replied.

"Why? Cause I'm drinking a beer?"

"Yes, that may have something to do with it,"

"What if I said I'm sorry and won't do it again?"

"You just had your chance and there are no more."

"You mean you're going to throw away our friendship over one beer?" he asked in unbelief.

I replied, "You haven't lived through the hell I have, and I'm not taking any chances. Don't call me or talk to me again. Goodbye."

It was years later that the Lord confirmed that I had made the right choice. I was an RN in ICU and met a former schoolmate. I asked about her life. She said she had married Rodney, but their marriage had lasted only six months. He was a drunk and had beat her repeatedly, always saying he was sorry afterward and promising he wouldn't do it again.

As I listened to her story, I was thankful I had obeyed the Spirit of God way back then and had not yielded to ungodly persuasion. As I thought more about this former classmate, I realized that by not getting involved with Rodney, God had helped me avoid a trap surely set for me by Satan. And I thanked God for wisdom and deliverance from another potentially horrible situation.

Admiring Lowell at his high school
graduation (ages 15 and 17)

7

YOUNG LOVE

When I was 14 years old, I met Lowell Graber. Little did I know that he would be my husband. Lowell was seeing a girlfriend of mine at the time. She wanted me to meet her new boyfriend, so they had stopped at our house in Centreville. While Lowell seemed nice enough, I was not impressed. It was a week or so later when he showed up on my doorstep, jilted and broken-hearted. I told him not to feel bad; he wasn't the first and would not be the last.

After that day, Lowell continued dropping by to see me. He would often sit and watch TV. I later learned that he didn't have a TV at home. He was a quiet and reserved kind of guy. He was respectful, attended church and did not cuss, drink or smoke. He was raised in a Mennonite home. Due to my past, I was very cautious and selective when it came to boyfriends. Although my father had done many sexual things to me, I considered myself a virgin still; by the grace of God, the abuse had not gone as far as intercourse.

I started dating Lowell when I was fifteen years old. Every Sunday, Lowell and I attended his family's Mennonite church together. I was even baptized there. I did date a few other boys now and then, but none compared to Lowell.

As our relationship grew, we spent more and more time together. Our friendship deepened quite rapidly. By the time I was 17 and Lowell was 19, we were sure we were meant for each other. I made it a point to tell Lowell about my childhood, not glossing over the traumatic events that had taken place or my family's dysfunctional lifestyle.

I felt, due to my upbringing, that I was not good enough to marry Lowell, since I was nothing but a bastard. He, at first, thought I was making it all up or had watched too many soap operas. He had never heard of this kind of deviant lifestyle and was shocked, to say the least.

Years later, Lowell told me that the first time he had come to see me, I was babysitting my little half-brother, Jake. As he observed me that day, the thought had occurred to him that I would make a good wife and mother for our children. As far as he was concerned, from there on, it was a done deal!

I was a baton twirler in the Centreville HS marching band, 1966-1970, and twirled fire and flags at football halftime shows.

When I was 17, my folks were evicted from the house in Centreville and had to move yet another time. I had a part-time job waitressing at a little diner uptown and did not want to move with them. As I began looking for a room to rent, a local neighbor offered me the opportunity to live with them. In exchange for room and board, I would babysit their son now and then. So in August, 1970, I left home and moved in with that neighbor. I was now a senior in high school.

At school, I was in the band and twirled a baton. During half-time at one football game, I twirled fire, and another time, flags. I was outgoing and friendly in school, but I never shared with friends anything about my past. I continued attending church and was involved with the youth group.

Without the supervision or guidance of my parents, my physical relationship with Lowell grew more intense. That fall I discovered that I was expecting a baby.

After sharing the situation with my mother, she advised me against getting married or even keeping the baby. She knew how to make me abort and offered me pills. Somewhat startled by her offer, I refused to take them, saying, "No. Even if Lowell doesn't want to get married, I will keep my baby and raise him alone."

At 17, I knew I needed to take responsibility for my actions. Furthermore, knowing that abortion was wrong (as well as illegal at that time), I would not even consider it. Two wrongs did not make a right. I was sorry for having yielded to my flesh and felt so

Lowell and I on our wedding day
November 21, 1970

ashamed. But I knew the baby within me was a human being, and I believed that abortion was murder.

After talking with our pastor, Lowell and I went before our church, publicly confessing our sin. We were asked to repent before the congregation, which we did, asking for forgiveness. The congregation then voted whether or not to accept us. We were forgiven.

Lowell and I were married November 21, 1970. I was 17 years old, three months pregnant, and

Mom and I on my wedding day!

Lowell was 19. We were married at Clinton Brick Mennonite Church. Warren, my step-father, walked me down the aisle.

I knew Lowell's parents were disappointed. They feared that I'd be like my parents and were concerned about my dysfunctional family background. They were also afraid that our marriage would not last, causing a lot of heartache for everyone, especially their son. At the time, I resented being judged for my parents' actions.

As I grew older, however, I fully understood their initial concerns. I believed I was an exception to what usually happens to children like me, and I set out to prove myself. I was determined to be a good wife and mother, but I did not know how. My parents obviously did not set a good example for me to follow.

As a newlywed, I read many Christian books about the husband and wife relationship and about raising children. I also read my Bible daily. I closely watched godly women and was mentored by some of them. By their example and teaching, I learned how to raise my children. I was far from a perfect wife or parent, but I had such a deep desire to honor God and serve Him.

PREGNANCY HELPLINE VOLUNTEER

In recent years, Father God called me to volunteer doing ultrasounds at a local Pregnancy Helpline. For years, I had carried shame about being pregnant before I was married. Because I had repented and asked forgiveness, I knew that God had taken my shame. But I could not seem to forgive myself.

Father God's plan was to use my former shame for His honor and glory by exchanging it for His righteousness. I had a story to share, and He knew how closely I would relate to the scared and confused girls I would meet decades later. I had been in their shoes and had experienced their shame. But now I was set free! *"There is therefore now no condemnation to those who are in Christ Jesus, who do not walk according to the flesh, but according to the Spirit"* *(Romans 8:1).* I realized I was treasured. *"The Lord delights in those who fear Him, who put their hope in His unfailing love" (Psalm 147:11 NIV).* I had mercy and compassion for them, knowing that even when things may look hopeless, Father God is still our hope.

LOVED BY AUNT VERA

As I look back over my life and think of the women who most impacted me, my Aunt Vera is at the top of my list. She was my father's oldest sister. When I was a young girl, I visited her often. She gave me something my mother with four children did not have—time for one-on-one and undivided attention. My father would sometimes take me to Elkhart with him. We would leave early in the morning; I would be dropped off at Aunt Vera's to spend the day while he went to work. Occasionally, I stayed a couple of days.

This was my happy place. I played with her neighbor girls, often roller skating on the sidewalks. Aunt Vera and I also did crafts together. Her home was clean, tidy, and adorned with pretty things she liked to set around. She was married to Uncle Diz, but I always kept him at a distance. I was shy around him, never getting to know him well. Besides, Uncle Diz and my father liked to drink together.

As I grew older and visited Aunt Vera less, I wrote her lots of letters, and she wrote back to me. She always remembered my birthday, giving me a little something like a coloring book and new box of crayons or a novel to read. I loved to visit her every chance I got, and that continued even after I was married and had my own children. Through the years, I never forgot the time and special attention she lavished on me.

As Aunt Vera aged, she developed health problems and was nearly blind. I brought her to our home at one point to care for her. I loved her dearly. She enjoyed fishing in our pond behind our house. She would cast out the line, and I would let her know when the bobber went down, and then she would pull in the fish. She got so excited!

Aunt Vera's mind began playing tricks on her. Even though she was not wealthy, she was convinced that I was stealing money from her and became paranoid. I cried and cried about that. I loved her so much and never would have stolen a thing from her. Because I was so broken-hearted, Lowell would not let me keep her with us any longer. So I called her daughter, Barbara, and we took Aunt Vera there.

Vera's son, Earl, also had health issues. So Barbara moved Aunt Vera back to her own home and invited Earl to move in with her. That proved to be the best solution for Vera, who was back in familiar territory. She and Earl helped each other and lived together for quite some time.

On the days I came to visit Aunt Vera, I did whatever chores needing doing, such as raking leaves, washing windows, cleaning her house, or tarring the garage roof. She still enjoyed outings, so I would take her shopping and out to eat. I also became her personal stylist, cutting her hair and giving her a permanent from time to time. We just enjoyed being together. I asked her one day while washing her windows why she wanted them washed

Aunt Vera, my father's sister, invested
lots of time and attention in my life.

since she was blind and couldn't see them. She
replied, "Because I know they are clean and sparkly,
and that makes me happy." It blessed me to serve
her and do whatever I could to bring her joy.

After fracturing her hip in a fall one day, Aunt
Vera ended up in a nursing home. She was placed
there temporarily for rehab, but she was never able
to walk much after that. So Earl then moved into
the nursing home, too. They were inseparable.

Aunt Vera continued to decline in health and
eventually passed away. We were all heartbroken. I
had the privilege of doing her hair one last time for

her funeral. Surprisingly, I was asked to conduct the funeral service as well. But before her funeral could take place, Earl also passed away. So I was asked to preach both funerals, which were then combined.

I had never done a funeral! However, if I could do one funeral, I guess I could do two; why not? What an honor it was to bring closure to my dear Aunt Vera's life, laying her to rest alongside her beloved son, Earl.

This apparently started a trend, because I was asked to preach my Uncle Glen's funeral a few short months later. But I thank God for the time I had with Aunt Vera and for her deep love for me, especially during the period of my life marked by much heartache and turmoil.

DESPISE NOT THE DAY OF SMALL BEGINNINGS

The first year after we were married, Lowell and I lived in Detroit, Michigan. Lowell was attending RETS Electronic School. It was a huge transition, moving from a small village community to a big inner-city. I enrolled at Detroit Southwestern my senior year of high school. The school was 98 percent black, and because I was a little white girl, I felt rather conspicuous.

At the start of school each day, the doors were chained shut from the inside. This was during the 70's when riots were taking place in big cities. I remember asking, "What if there is a fire? How will we get out?" The principal told me not to worry because he had the key to unlock the door.

I was determined to finish high school, so I decided to stay, even though I was fearful. There were multiple challenges.

One day in study hall, several students surrounded me, demanding I give them money, but I had none. The one and only teacher supervising us was busy on the other side of the room. Then some of the boys threatened to rape me and proceeded to unzip my jumper. I managed to get away, running into the hall and right into the principal. He asked me what the problem was. I was an emotional wreck, crying hysterically. The boys were expelled from school. The principal took me home that day and told me that those boys would come after me to get even.

After that incident, I was even more frightened. So I changed my schedule and daily routine, studying in the counselor's office. One day they spotted me, pointed, and yelled, "There's that white bitch!" I took off running. Thankfully, I never saw them again.

In 1970, girls were not allowed to attend school while pregnant, even if they were married. So I was transferred to William Booth Memorial Home for unwed mothers. Girls there were known only by their first names and last initial.

I actually finished my classes early, graduating with honors. I received my diploma from Detroit Southwestern High School. Since I was the first married girl to graduate from there, a newspaper article was published, complete with a picture of myself and our baby, Joe.

Being young and having a baby made things really tight financially. I like to say we lived off love. Lowell and I grew up together it seemed, learning to depend on each other. We did meet some older couples in Detroit who kind of looked out for us.

We lived in Detroit only one year before moving back to White Pigeon and renting an upstairs apartment. There were many hardships to come, and we were still immature. Although we had a lot of growing up to do with plenty of hard knocks ahead, Father God never left me. I did not know much spiritually, but I possessed a fierce hunger and thirst to know more.

Our first house in a back alley of Detroit.
I don't despise the day of small beginnings.

My HS senior picture, 1971

Since Lowell had been raised in a Christian home, he had far more Bible knowledge than I did, which, it seemed to me, he took for granted. But because I had lived through hell and desired a better life, I longed to know God and His peace and love. I kept searching for the right way to live and for someone to mentor me. God was faithful to send people to influence us. We found a church and began to grow in our walk with Christ.

In our first six years of marriage, we had three sons—Joseph, Joshua, and Jonathan. By the time I was 23, I thought our family was complete. Little did I know what God had planned.

It was during this time, that a lot of painful emotions began to surface from deep inside me. I had so very many questions that needed answers. I called my mother and asked her to come over, intending to confront her about the past. I had to know why she had done the things she did, which had devastated my life. Sometimes, we have to confront our past before we can move forward.

Mom and I talked openly that day, and she did answer my questions. She said she wished she could change things, but since she couldn't go back, she asked for my forgiveness. She confessed that she had basically been driven by fear, the fear of being alone. She reassured me that she did not plan for Willis to kill my father and then run off with him.

A thousand pounds were lifted from my shoulders during our time together, and we made peace with one another. My mother had many problems and heartaches from her past as well, but sin had become the norm for her life.

Even though we came to an understanding, we did not always get along or see eye to eye. I was especially careful not to allow her to interfere in my marriage.

One day she asked, "Why do you always go to Lowell about everything, even when I ask you to do something?"

My answer was, "Because he is more my husband than you are my mother. Lowell and I are one now."

SHIELD OF FAITH

One day, my mother called and invited me to come over and help her hang wallpaper in her bathroom and hallway. When I arrived, she and my younger half-brother, Jacob, were arguing. She was in a fit of rage and had grabbed a butcher knife. I told her to put it down. It seemed she didn't hear me.

I finally shouted, "In Jesus' name, put it down!" I then walked outside, but she came after me, trying to strike me with her fist. I kept repeating, "I plead the blood of Jesus! Satan, I take authority over you!"

She continued swinging her fist at me, but it was as if I had a protective shield around me that she could not penetrate.

I kept repeating, "In the name of Jesus!" Suddenly, she dropped to the ground and began slithering like a snake, her tongue darting in and out of her mouth. I knew then that she was demon-possessed, and the demon was manifesting itself. This lasted maybe two to three minutes. Then, just as suddenly, she jumped up and ran back into the house.

Giving her time to settle down, I called Duane, a friend of mine with experience in casting out demons. I explained the situation and asked if he would help my mom. He agreed and asked me to bring her to his house and he and his wife would minister to her.

At that point in my Christian walk, I did not yet know how to deal with such a situation. I told Mom what she had done. She did not even remember it. She was totally unaware of what had just happened, but she was willing to see Duane. Through the years, my mother had been involved in many activities that opened the door to the enemy.

I dropped Mom off at Duane's house. He said he would take her home after the ministry session and call me with a report. When he called me some time later, he reported that he had cast multiple demons out of Mom.

By the grace of God, she was set free, and I never saw her manifest again. What I did see was a real change in my mother. She grew spiritually and began hungering and thirsting after righteousness. She also began attending church regularly and was baptized.

There are 23 Bible verses about demons and casting them out. What demons could do in Bible times, they can still do today. *"And these signs will accompany those who believe: In my name, they will drive out demons; they will speak in new tongues" (Mark 16:17 NIV).*

My mother received Jesus into her heart as her Lord and Savior and was baptized at a family camp through the Florence Brethren Church. She truly was born again, and her life was transformed. She read her Bible and listened to good preaching tapes as well. She especially liked to go to revival meetings. She even witnessed to some of her family and friends and prayed for them. Her sister, Bertha, once commented to me about the wonderful changes she saw in Mom.

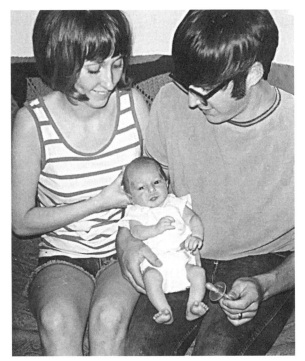

Lowell and I, newlyweds, with Joe,
our firstborn

TRUSTING GOD TO LEAD

As Lowell and I continued to grow spiritually, God began sending people across my path who told me about the Baptism of the Holy Spirit. At first, I was frightened and unsure. I kept seeking for the truth in God's Word and praying for clarification.

In 1977, we moved to Sherwood, Michigan, due to Lowell's work. We were there for only one year, but we made many good friends. I started selling Home Interiors and Gifts at in-home parties (like Tupperware). It gave us a little extra money, and because Lowell watched the boys those two or three evenings each week, we didn't have to pay a babysitter. Looking back, I realize that was when I became comfortable with public speaking. I enjoyed getting out with women for a couple of hours while also contributing to our family income.

I became acquainted with some Pentecostal folks during that time, and we found them really fascinating. They inspired me and increased my hunger for God.

One evening following a Home Interiors party, I stopped at a Mr. Donut shop to see my cousin, Barbara. She introduced me to a couple of guys who were in the area having Bible studies. They were very bold for God.

The first thing they asked is, "Have you been baptized in the Holy Spirit?"

I was not sure what they meant and was afraid to discuss it. So they asked me, "Who is the author of fear?" I knew Satan was and said so. Then they instructed me about the Holy Spirit and gave me scripture and verses to look up. While I did not receive the baptism that night, I certainly had a lot of new information in my heart to ponder and consider.

About that time, Lowell and I planned to move again. We put our house up for sale. It sold for full price within one week. People from Albuquerque, New Mexico, had driven by and seen the sign. Because the house we were purchasing was not yet ready, we lived for three months in Burr Oak,

Michigan, where we rented an old farmhouse from some friends.

One significant incident stands out in my memory from our time there. Our youngest son, Jonathan, who was approximately two years old, began choking on something he had picked up from the floor. When I found him, he was limp and blue. My heart was racing. "Dear Jesus, help me!"

Just the day before while looking through a magazine, I had read instruction on the Heimlich maneuver. While I was reading that article, the thought occurred to me that someday I may need to know this. I had no idea it would be the very next day! It was Father God's perfect timing, giving me the knowledge I needed to save my son. God seemed to always be preparing me for the next step in life.

Our next move was to Paris, Michigan, in the spring of 1979. A friend, Verna, came to welcome me to the neighborhood. She also shared with me about the Baptism of the Holy Spirit, leaving me with a small pamphlet entitled, "Welcome to the Family," by Kenneth Copeland (1979). By that time I knew God was definitely speaking to me.

I eagerly read the pamphlet after she left and immediately followed the instructions. By faith, I received the baptism of the Holy Spirit and spoke in another tongue, a new language that flowed fluently from me. I laughed and laughed for hours. God spoke to my heart and said, *"You love righteousness and hate wickedness; therefore God, your God set you above your companions by anointing you with the oil of joy."* I did not even realize at the time that this was a scripture in both the Old and New Testaments *(Psalm 45:7 NIV and Hebrews 1:9 NIV)*.

This new experience opened up a whole new realm to me, and I began to grow spiritually by leaps and bounds. I had stepped from religion into a personal relationship with Jesus Christ. I began to hear His voice within me, leading and guiding me into all truth. I also received power to witness and share with others.

Lowell and I started attending a Pentecostal or "charismatic" church. We listened to tapes and teachings that encouraged faith in God's Word, furthering our spiritual growth and maturity. Today, I'm so thankful that Lowell and I started when we were young, over 45 years ago, to hide God's Word in our hearts and renew our minds.

JAIL MINISTRY

My mother sent us her copy of the local Three Rivers newspaper so we could keep up on the news from back home. One day while reading it, I recognized the name of a childhood friend of my youngest brother, Nathan. As a young boy, John would come to our home to hang out with Nathan. I remember playfully ruffling his hair and saying, "Wish you were older. You're a cutie." Now John was grown and in the Centreville jail for the murder of a man at a local bar.

Father God spoke to my heart, "I want you to write to him, and tell him about Me." I sat right down and wrote a long letter. I explained first who I was and then proceeded to tell him about Jesus. I told him about the love of God and His forgiveness and about repentance. I sealed the letter, prayed over it, walked it to our mailbox, and placed it inside. Walking back to the house, my head raged with accusations. He will think you're a nut! He won't even remember you! I walked back and forth several times, trying to decide whether or not to mail it. Then it occurred to me that these doubts were from the enemy, attempting to discourage me. I left the letter in the mailbox.

Within a few short days, I was surprised to receive a letter back from John. He told me he'd hit rock bottom and had prayed, "God, if you are real, I need You. Send someone to tell me about You." It was the very next day that he had received my letter. I thank God for the prompting of the Holy Spirit and that I was obedient. In his letter to me, John shared how he had received Jesus as his Lord and Savior. Then he had passed my letter to other cells, and several more inmates were born again. They all desired to know more and wanted a Bible study.

That's how I got started writing to 15 men in jail about Jesus. I did not talk about my personal life, only sharing about Jesus and scripture. The inmates would write, asking me questions. I bought a case of Bibles and took them to the jail on a visit. Due to them having hard covers, the prison was not going to allow the Bibles to be distributed. So we ripped off the covers! The sheriff could not believe that I would rip covers off of brand new Bibles. I told him, "It's the inside they need, not the outside."

I replied to every letter the inmates sent to me, and I also prayed for them. It was my ministry during that season. Sometimes, my husband and our pastor would accompany me on my visits with them, as the Lord directed us. This lasted a couple of years, and just as it had started, it slowly subsided as the inmates moved on or were transferred. I was always open and honest with the inmates, telling them that all I had to offer them was Jesus and His Word. Someday when I get to heaven, I will know the impact of that ministry and the lives that were changed. Nothing we do for Jesus is a waste of time.

FAVOR IN THE MARKET PLACE

We had lived in Paris, Michigan, about three years when again, due to Lowell's work with irrigation, we considered moving. Lowell actually had seven job offers, so we prayed for God's perfect will of which to choose and where to move.

At the time, we were buying a house on five acres, and we were not sure what to do with that house. Should we rent it or put it up for sale?

Lowell and I both had dreams one night that brought confirmation and unity about what to do. We both believed that our pastor's family was to live in our house for one year, rent free. Although we were still making payments on the house, we were convinced that we were not to charge them rent. We talked to them and found out how right we were. We had no idea that they also needed to move and had been praying about what they were going to do.

They were waiting for the Lord's answer when we presented what Father God had spoken to our hearts. At first they declined, but they soon came to the conclusion that this was God's answer to their prayers for a house. This was a big step of faith for us to say the least!

So in the spring of 1982, we packed up and moved south to Schoolcraft, Michigan where we rented a big old farmhouse for $300 a month. Our payments on the house up north were also $300 a month. This was a tremendous stretch for us financially because I was not employed at the time. We couldn't even afford a telephone.

To keep warm, and due to the high heating cost, we cut wood for the winter. As a matter of fact, even though the house was big, all three of our boys slept downstairs in sleeping bags in the living room where it was warmer. They thought we were camping! Regardless of the inconvenience to us financially, we knew we had been obedient to God's leading.

We learned a lot during that year. Our hearts were fixed on trusting in the Lord. Family and friends alike questioned our choice regarding the pastor and his family, but we were not shaken. While living in Schoolcraft, we had many opportunities to minister and to share the love of Jesus and His Word with neighbors and newfound friends. It was a time of both challenge and growth.

In 1983, we had an opportunity to buy another house at a discount, since it was being repossessed. It was located close to where we were currently living. Lowell took me to see it. The house was

Before picture of our fixer-upper house

covered with black tarpaper, and the weeds were as high as the front door. I told Lowell it was ugly as sin. We went inside where we found dead rats and a ladder where the stairs should have been. Along with having no flooring or drywall, at least half the windows were missing. It was a terrible sight! As we walked through the house envisioning future rooms, both of us could see its potential through the eyes of faith. We also knew what that house would require—loads and loads of hard work.

We asked a cousin of Lowell's, a contractor, to take a look at the house. He said the walkout basement alone was worth more than the $15,000 they were asking. Besides that, the house was sitting on five acres. So we prayed about what to offer. Lowell felt the Lord had told him $7,500. Even though I thought it was crazy, we made the offer. They countered at $10,000 with a three-year land contract and a balloon payment due at the end of the three years.

We took the challenge and bought the house and began to fix it up enough to make it livable.

We now had three house payments, making things even tighter financially. We knew that we needed to get rid of one of our three houses!

Instead, we moved into the foreclosed house when all the windows were in and the staircase was done. Drywall was on one side of the walls and studs were on the other. We purchased only bottom cabinets for the kitchen temporarily and had one usable bathroom

After picture of our completed house

with a door. Our floors were just bare sub-flooring, so I painted them. Our only bedroom with a door became Lowell's and mine. We did all the dry-walling and finishing work ourselves. It was quite rough looking. Our Christian friends asked, "How can you live like that?" And even my mother commented that we were living like a bunch of hillbillies.

After one year, the seller came back to us with an offer. If we would pay off the land contract right then, we could have it for $7,500. We rejoiced, knowing Lowell had heard correctly from the Spirit of God!

We continued fixing up our house as we could afford it, a little at a time. After discovering that there were natural springs behind our house, we dug a pond. The pond was 100 feet by 200 feet and ten feet deep; we stocked it with hybrid bluegill and bass. Our sons, along with their friends, enjoyed many fun days of swimming in the pond in the summer and ice skating in the winter. We also added a large wrap-around porch on three sides of the house.

People often commented that our yard looked like a park. We eventually had weddings there as well as church picnics, reunions, and baptisms in the pond.

We lived there for 18 years. Lowell and I always believed that house was the evidence and fruit of our obedience to God, our blessing for allowing the pastor's family to live in our northern house rent free. We were learning many things living by faith and continued to grow spiritually. When we sold this home ourselves with no realtor, we got our asking price of $149,000. We reaped a great return from our investment in the marketplace and reaped even more spiritually.

YOU SHALL LIVE AND NOT DIE

A few years ago, Lowell had an abscessed tooth and was taking prescription antibiotics and pain meds. His severe pain was not subsiding, so more meds were prescribed. Then he began complaining of neck pain, so he went to our chiropractor for an adjustment. He continued to be in pain and began having difficulty swallowing, even soft oatmeal. He felt good enough to go to church one Sunday, and when service was over, we requested prayer for his neck.

After church, we went to visit his parents, returning home later in the evening. Lowell seemed to be feeling progressively worse as the day wore on. When we arrived home, I noticed he was unstable and almost passing out. It was time to take him to the local hospital and get a diagnosis.

The hospital staff X-rayed his neck and prescribed a muscle relaxer and pain meds. When I happened to mention that he had been having dental issues and was taking antibiotics to be proactive, they decided to do soft tissue X-rays as well. We were assured that we would receive results the next day, so we returned home.

Lowell slept well that night, thinking, as he woke up the next morning, that he might be able to go to work. But we soon realized that wasn't happening, so he just continued sleeping.

I received a call from the radiologist telling me that Lowell had a retro-pharyngeal abscess and must be taken to the hospital immediately. The doctor further told me that my husband's airway was closing off; that's why he was having difficulty swallowing and was experiencing neck pain. I stayed calm so as not to alarm Lowell, woke him up, and told him that we needed to go to the hospital for further testing. As he got ready, I prepared an overnight bag for him.

1998 - Ben and I visiting Lowell,
who was hospitalized for a retropharyngeal abscess

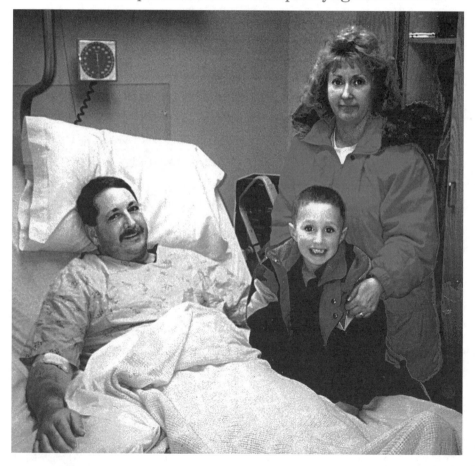

In the meantime, it had begun snowing heavily—the beginning of a blizzard. I called our grown sons and pastors, asking them to meet us at the hospital. Once we arrived, I seated Lowell in the waiting room and signed him in. I explained to the nurse that we had been sent there by the doctor due to a retro-pharyngeal abscess and that his X-rays would soon be there. I was told to take a seat and wait.

Our sons and pastors arrived to support us, but we soon sent them all back home because the snow was still coming down heavily. I went back to the desk repeatedly, emphasizing how serious our case was, but it was like the hospital staff didn't hear me. Each time, I was told to go back to the waiting room and wait. They were very busy, and the waiting room was full. We endured a three-hour wait before he was finally seen in the emergency room. I tried to remain calm, praying constantly.

The X-rays never arrived, so an MRI was ordered because they had no verification of what I had told them. The MRI confirmed that Lowell did have a retro-pharyngeal abscess and that his airway was closing.

The staff jumped into action and called in the surgical team. As the surgeon and anesthesiologist were standing next to Lowell's gurney, they instructed us to say our good-byes. They were not sure if Lowell would make it through surgery. Fear tried to grip my heart, but I resisted. Having filled my heart with His Word, God had prepared me for this moment. Lowell, of course, was listening to what they said and he had tears running down his cheeks.

I said to Lowell, "You will live and not die! I will not stop praying and interceding for you."

I told the doctor, "God be with you" and kissed Lowell as he was wheeled away into surgery. It was early morning by that time, and the waiting room was now empty. I paced and prayed, declaring the promises of God over and over. My strength and confidence were in God's Word.

Two hours later, the doctor came to tell me that he had successfully inserted a tube to keep Lowell's airway open. And after viewing the abscess, they had made the decision to treat him at the hospital using strong IV antibiotics. He also shared that because Lowell was combative, they had placed him in four-point leather restraints.

I went in to see him, and the nurse shared that the respiratory therapist had actually held him down while they restrained him. The medication was making him wild, and he had been hitting and throwing nurses around.

Once I arrived, I held his hand. Using sign language, he spelled into my palm the letters *"Get me out of here!"* I released the restraints and sat next to the bed, leaning over onto his chest. He settled down after that and was fine, allowing the nurse to remove the breathing tube from his throat. It took a week in the hospital for Lowell to fully recover.

After that incident, we heard of others who had died from the very same thing. Infection in the teeth can be dangerous; sometimes traveling in soft tissues to the brain, heart, and throat, which can be life threatening. We thanked God for wisdom and for healing Lowell.

My mother's first four children:
(back) Alvin and Harriet,
(front) Marie and Kay

FINDING MARIE

For many years, Lowell and I were given opportunities to travel extensively due to business conventions in his field of work. He was a salesman for an irrigation company. Many times, we hired someone we knew well to stay with our boys. Sometimes we even took a few extra days, traveling in the destination area and enjoying needed quality time together. With all expenses paid, we counted these trips a huge blessing. The conventions took place every year or two. Occasionally, we took the boys along for a family vacation.

One year as we were driving home, I suggested that we look up my half-sister, Elizabeth Marie. She had been adopted as an infant and was the youngest of the four children that my mother had given up. I had never met her, but I had been told that she was bitter about the adoption, refusing even to see family who had tried to contact her. I

Marie and I on the day we met
at her home in Hutchinson, Kanas

asked God to make a way where there was no way and for her to receive me. While we were still on the road, I felt strongly compelled to contact her, so I got her phone number from a relative. I called, but she was not home, so I called again later. When she answered, I explained who I was, assuring her that as her half-sister and a Christian, I meant her no harm. I further stated that it was not my intent to disrupt her or her family, but if I could just stop by and meet her, we would then be on our way.

She hesitated but then replied, "I always wanted a sister. Yes, come." Thank you, Jesus, for answered prayer! It was nothing short of a miracle; only God can change a person's heart.

It was several hours before we arrived at her home. When she came out to greet us, I stared at her in amazement. She looked just like her two older sisters, Harriet and Kay. Even her mannerisms were the same as theirs. She invited us in. Wanting some time to get acquainted with me, she had even prepared a meal for us. I was shocked, but my heart was rejoicing!

That evening as we talked and shared our stories, she asked many questions. She wondered how any mother could give up her six-month-old baby; she felt rejected. As we talked, Father God enlightened me. I then explained to Marie that while I was sure of what I was about to share, I had no idea how I knew it, except by the Spirit of God. I knew there were times when Mother held me as an infant that she would just weep and weep. God showed me at that moment, while sitting with Marie, that since I was the next child born to her, our mother was actually weeping for the little baby girl she had given up. I just knew in my heart it was true, and I intended to ask my mother for confirmation when I returned home.

My half-sister and I connected really well that night. I found out that she preferred to be called Marie. She had struggled for years with rejection and heartache. She shared that a conservative Mennonite family had adopted her and that she'd had a good upbringing. I even got to meet her adoptive mother and father, and I could tell they were prosperous people. I shared with Marie that I believed she was much better off being adopted by them, than I had been with my parents. I told her about some of the trauma I had experienced as a child.

After returning home, I called my mother and gave her an update on our trip. Soon after, while showing her pictures of Marie, I shared Marie's story. And yes, I had been correct. Many times while rocking me, my mother had wept for the baby girl she had given away. She marveled that I knew this. We both agreed it was a revelation from God.

Mom was thrilled that I had found Marie and wanted desperately to talk to her. Marie had already informed me that she would not talk to Mom on the phone. She was not yet ready for that, but she was open to a letter. Mom worried that she could not convey in a letter all the things she longed to say directly to Marie. She wanted to touch Marie's heart. We prayed, asking God to help her and for love to flow to Marie.

Mom did write the letter, explaining to Marie the circumstances surrounding her adoption. She also assured her daughter that she was very much loved and how she had longed for her over the years. She also asked Marie to forgive her. When Marie received the letter, it not only touched her heart, but it answered many of her questions as well. Bitterness and rejection were defeated, and Mom was forgiven. Mom had so hoped to meet Marie in person. Unfortunately, that never happened.

A little over a week later—December, 1984—my mother suddenly died. Thanks be to God that He granted Mom the opportunity to express her love to Marie and to ask for and receive forgiveness. Just prior to her death, Mom had been diagnosed with Parkinson's disease. Marie told me recently that although it's been many years, she has kept that letter as a continued reassurance of her birth mother's love.

MOM'S DEATH

Mom and I had gone to a funeral together. My dad's first wife, Virginia (Chester and Ronnie's mother) had died. My mom knew her and wanted to attend. On the way home, she talked about the funeral, the people she saw there, and about how things went. She then cautiously asked, "Would it upset you if I told you right now how I want my funeral?"

I replied, "Why no, we are all going to die sometime. Who knows, I may die before you."

Although she disagreed that I would die first, she proceeded to give me details for her funeral. First, she wanted to be buried in Arthur, Illinois beside her parents. My stepfather knew of her wish, but Mom was quite certain that he would not honor her request, wanting her buried near him instead. She made me promise that I would do all that I could to honor her request. I promised her that I would remind my stepfather of her wish, but ultimately, it was his decision to make as her husband, not mine. It then came to me—it won't be long now! I wondered what that meant. Surely my mother wasn't about to die?

Then I heard, "Tell your mom now that you love her."

Again I thought, "Why? She knows I love her." But I chose obedience, and reaching over, patted her on the leg. "Mama, you know I love you."

She replied, "Yes, and I love you."

A few short days later, she died of a blood clot to her heart. She had not felt well that day, and my brother, Jake, had found her at home on the sofa. Jake was hysterical when he called me. I told him to call an ambulance and I would come as soon as I could. I wanted to pray with my immediate family first. So Lowell and I joined hands with our three sons and prayed. As soon as I began to pray aloud, I heard, "She's with me." I stopped, knowing she was already with Father God. He placed a song in my heart that carried me through the preparations and the funeral.

Last photo of my mother and me together

O victory in Jesus,
    my Savior, forever!
He sought me and bought me
    with His redeeming blood;
He loved me ere I knew Him,
    and all my love is due Him.
He plunged me to victory
    beneath the cleansing flood
    (Bartlett, 1939)

When Mom repented of her sins, the atoning blood of Jesus cleansed her, so Mama was now home with Jesus, totally free at last, 20 years after my dad's death. In His remarkable grace, God had allowed me the opportunity to tell each of my parents that I loved them shortly before they passed.

My sister, Shirley, is congratulating
me on my graduation from KVCC
Nursing School in 1993.

CALLED TO NURSING

Over the span of several years, Lowell and I
continued to fix up our home in Schoolcraft, adding
landscaping as well. At one point, Lowell used a
bulldozer to level out the yard, pushing dirt from
around the pond into the uneven areas of the yard. In
the process, a few sapling trees had been broken off,
leaving only ragged, splintered edges sticking up.

At one point, we purchased a mini motorcycle for the boys, which they enjoyed riding on our five acres. Like most parents, we took extra precautions for their safety, giving us some peace of mind. We required helmets, long pants, and that they never ride double. One day, I saw our oldest son riding the mini cycle with the neighbor boy, Phil, on the back. I went over and reminded Joe of the rules. He insisted that his dad had given him permission. I told him that he better not be lying to me because I would be checking with his dad later. Joe knew if he was lying, he would be disciplined.

I then went behind the house to put away the garden hose. Suddenly, a blood curdling scream filled my ears. I ran around the house to find Joe stumbling towards me with a gaping, bloody hole in his pants, near his groin. Phil was with Joe but appeared to be fine. He explained that Joe had hit a bump, dumping him off the cycle. I sent Phil home, then carefully walked Joe to our car and placed him in the passenger side, tipping the seat back to get a better view of his injury. Even though Joe was in a lot of pain, he kept demanding that I pray, which I did—hard and fast. He told me that when he fell off the cycle, he had landed on one of the broken saplings with splintered, ragged edges, but he had managed to pull himself free.

The neighbor man had been outside, and hearing the screams, had staggered over to the car. When he came close, I could tell he was intoxicated. He said, "You need to call an ambulance and get a blanket so he doesn't go into shock." I bolted for the house;

the phone was ringing as I stepped inside. It was my friend, Carol, and I quickly explained that I couldn't talk because Joe was injured and I needed to call for an ambulance. Before hanging up, she asked how she could help. I gave her Lowell's number and asked her to contact him so he could get to the hospital ASAP. After phoning for an ambulance, I called our pastor who agreed to meet me at the hospital. Heeding the neighbor's advice, I retrieved a blanket before running back outside to Joe, and I prayed some more. Joe was frightened and believed he was dying. The ambulance arrived, got him loaded, and off we went. I was in the back with my son, still

Joe at age 13

praying. Whenever I attempted to answer questions the ambulance attendant was asking, Joe would tell me in a panic, "Just pray!"

When we arrived at the hospital, our pastor and Lowell were already there. Joe was rushed in, ahead of everyone else. The halls were lined with drunks and sick people. Back in the exam room, the nurses were scurrying around and asking lots of questions. But Joe wouldn't let them touch him until our pastor had prayed over him. Pastor prayed all right, loud enough that everyone there could have been healed.

They rushed Joe in for X-rays and CT scans. The doctor was already saying it was a miracle that Joe wasn't dead. A police officer had been dispatched to our house to dig up the sapling tree stump, which he brought to the hospital for the doctor to see. The sapling was as big around as a 50-cent piece. It had gone six to seven inches into Joe's groin, miraculously missing all his vital organs, as well as the aorta, the main artery in the abdomen. If the stick had impaled the aorta, Joe would have quickly bled to death. Joe told me later that whenever I had stopped praying, he could feel his spirit lifting out of his body and was sure he would have died, had I not kept praying.

Joe was admitted to the hospital, and his wound was kept open, needing to heal from the inside out. Three times a day, it was cleansed with Betadine and flushed with peroxide to wash out all the bark and dirt. One day, Josh and Jon went with me to the hospital to visit their brother. Upon our arrival, we were informed that Joe was being prepped for surgery because he had a high fever, signaling a possible infection. We went into Joe's room and prayed. God reminded me that every one of us had been sick the past week with the flu, except for Joe. Joe's high temp was from the flu, not an infection. After sharing my thoughts with the doctor, he agreed to wait 24 hours, but he warned me that if there was no change by that time, Joe must go into surgery. I agreed with his decision. By that evening, Joe's temperature had come down.

Day and night during Joe's hospital stay, we played healing scriptures from a cassette player at his bedside. The staff was amazed at the Bible knowledge he had at 13 years of age.

After one week, Joe was discharged to my care at home. His care included taking him for weekly follow-up appointments. Joe's doctor was an elderly, white-haired gentleman. He told me that he had been a doctor a long time, and because of that, he knows a nurse when he sees one. He looked directly at me and announced, "You are called to be a nurse." I argued with him that I could never do that. He simply replied, "Yes you can."

Every week for six weeks, the doctor continued to insist that I was called to be a nurse. But I had no confidence, and little self-esteem. "You'll never amount to anything" had echoed in my head for years.

Several weeks had passed when I saw an ad, asking for volunteers for a basic emergency course. Out of gratitude for the ambulance service and their help with Joe, I thought, "That's the least I can do."

So I volunteered, taking my first baby step of faith towards God's goal for me.

After passing basic training I was invited to be an EMT. The ambulance service would pay for further training. I was nervous that I wouldn't pass, wasting their funds. I studied hard and prayed that God would bring back to my remembrance what I needed to know. Amazingly, I passed. I volunteered as an EMT on the ambulance service for ten years. As my faith grew, I continued taking classes.

HEALING THE BROKEN-HEARTED

Shortly after Joe was healed, my cousin, Barbara, invited me to share Joe's story at a Bible study. I accepted even though I didn't know any of the people attending or anything about them. As I was nearing the end of Joe's story, I felt prompted to say that many there had deep penetrating wounds as well; and they, too, needed healing from the inside out. Further, it would take cleansing by the Word of God and forgiveness. I went on to say that covering up their wounds, rather than dealing with them, would cause them to get infected and fester, spreading toxins to other areas of their spirit. To my amazement, they all dropped to their knees, weeping and wailing. I certainly had not expected that. I didn't know quite what to do, so I just walked around laying hands on each of them and asking the Spirit of God to minister to their broken hearts. Once they regained their composure and were seated again, they all confessed that they had just come through a church split, leaving all of them broken and wounded. The Spirit of God showed up and did surgery on each and every heart that day.

In the meantime, it seemed I could not stop thinking about what Joe's doctor had repeatedly said to me, "You are called to be a nurse." Actually, my mother had harped at me and my sister for years, insisting that one of us should become a nurse. I always told her that it wasn't going to be me; I had no such desire. "Shirley can be a nurse but not me." However, Shirley insisted she didn't want to be a nurse either.

Mom had confessed to us that she always wanted to be a nurse, but school for her had been a difficult struggle. She attended school only through the sixth grade, which was typical for the Amish community. So she wanted at least one of her daughters to fulfill her dream.

And here, all these years later, God was nudging me, giving me a desire and the encouragement needed, to go to college for nursing. So at age 35, off I went to a local college to be tested to see if I could make it in the nursing program.

In 1990, I enrolled at Kalamazoo Valley Community College, starting with my prerequisites for the nursing program. I felt sad that my mother was gone and would not be there to cheer me on as I began this new adventure. She would have been so pleased and proud! But I consoled myself with the knowledge that there is a time and season for all things (Ecclesiastes 3:1). God was now showing me that this was the season for getting my nursing degree.

With three teenagers at home, working part-time, being older, and now taking college classes, the load was hard on me! I cared for elderly people in their homes through Homecare while I attended college. Lowell was very supportive and encouraged me to pursue my nursing degree. My instructors detected that I had gaps in my education, actually asking me if I had moved around a lot during my childhood. They were very helpful and worked closely with me.

My second year, I dropped back to part-time classes to care for my sister-in-law, Jean (Chester's wife), who was diagnosed with lung cancer. I considered it the school of real life, and I certainly learned a lot. I had the rest of my life to become a nurse, but Chet and Jean needed my help now. Jean was suffering with intense pain, and I knew her death was near. I remember telling Chet that he needed to release Jean and let her go. He cried and refused. "She is all I have left!"

He asked me to go home because if this was going to be her last night, he wanted to be alone with her. Later he told me he couldn't stop thinking about what I had said. So he went into the bedroom, took Jean's weak and thin body into his arms, and rocked her. He told her how much he loved her and that it was okay for her to go, assuring her he would be okay and would join her in heaven later. After a few hours, she opened her eyes, nodded at him, and took her final breath here on earth. He waited awhile, holding her and weeping, then phoned me to come saying, "It's over."

BONUS BLESSING

I graduated with honors in 1993, earning an Associates in Applied Science, Phi Theta Kappa Society. I passed my registered nursing boards on the first try. However, God had a bit of a surprise in store for us during my last semester. I found out that I was pregnant with our fourth child, meaning there would be a sixteen-year gap between my two youngest sons. I was in total denial. This just could not be possible! I went to a clinic and took a pregnancy test three times. I just knew it was wrong. I never considered abortion as an option. The women at the clinic asked, "Why do you think you can't be pregnant?"

"Because I'm 38 years old and have a 21-year-old son! People don't do this now!"

"Apparently you do," they replied.

When I told Lowell, he was happy and had no problem whatsoever with the idea. He said he felt like he was being given a second chance because he had been so busy working when our first three sons were young. When I told our three older boys, they were ecstatic. "We knew the old man was a stud!"

Jonathan observed, "Mom, you don't seem real happy." I told him that I was just trying to wrap my head around it, that I had other plans and was still in college.

Jon said, "I thought you loved kids."

"I do," I assured him.

He said, "I thought you loved us."

Again I said, "I do."

Family picture 1993: (front) Lowell, me holding
Ben, (back) Jon, Josh, and Joe

"We just want you to love this baby like you do
us. You are a great mom!"

I assumed that I would have to quit college, along
with nursing, and stay home. But Lowell would not
hear of it. He wanted me to continue and finish
getting my degree. He further assured me that I
could work part-time while the baby was little.

Our fourth son was born on October 21, 1992—
Benjamin David—named by his three big brothers. It
was a huge adjustment for us all, but we loved him

and adapted. As he grew, none of us could imagine life without him. We called him Our Bonus Blessing Ben.

Frankly, it was disappointing how some Christian people reacted, asking if we were going to raise him on our Social Security. I was honestly more ready for a child at 38 than I had ever been at 17. Some people acted like it was the end of our lives, as if it were terrible news, like a cancer diagnosis. I used these incidents as opportunities to remind people that children are blessings from the Lord. And I firmly believed it.

ANOTHER SON

After having Ben, because of the 16 year gap, I didn't want him raised like an only child. I reasoned that Ben should have a brother or sister so they could grow up together. So at 39 years of age I was pregnant again.

At 16 weeks, we discovered by ultrasound that the baby had no heartbeat. I was told that our fifth child was dead. I went into "nursing mode," asking with no emotion, "Now, what do we do?"

After learning my options, I chose to wait; I would deliver the baby naturally when my hormones dropped, causing my body to recognize that I was no longer pregnant. The nurses wanted to call Lowell and ask him to come get me, but I insisted that was not necessary. I was fine.

I left and immediately drove a few blocks away to my dear friend's home. I knocked on the door, and when Pam answered, I burst into tears. She wrapped her arms around me and cried with me. After we had sobbed together and dried our tears, she asked, "Why are we crying?" She was a true friend and loved me, crying when I cried even without yet knowing what was wrong. I told her about the baby; she let me talk, and then comforted me.

Later, just as I arrived home and stepped over the threshold, amazingly, my labor began. I was now in my safe place. Home. Our older boys went to a football game, and Lowell worked in the garage while Ben played quietly. It wasn't long. While alone in the bathroom, I delivered our fifth son, Abe. He had his thumb in his mouth just like my Jonathan did at his delivery. He had big blue eyes and looked much like our other boys. I called for Lowell, and he came in and knelt down by my side. We held our little Abe, prayed over him, and committed his spirit to the Lord. We cried and prayed some more, and then we kissed him, telling him how loved he was and how sorry I was that he could not stay with us.

I called the hospital and was instructed to come in because they wanted to check me over. We were to bring the fetus with us. We grabbed a large bath towel in case of bleeding and headed for the hospital with our tiny Abe. Our intent was to bring him back home and bury him ourselves.

By the time we arrived, I was hemorrhaging, and the towel was soaked with blood. They put me in a wheelchair and took me directly back to the emergency room. The doctor came in, and after examining me, said I needed a D&C. I presumed

I'd be taken to the operating room. The doctor said, "No, this will be quick and easy; we will do it here in the emergency room."

As a nurse, I was quite surprised. They gave me a Norco for pain prevention. Lowell took Ben out into the waiting room; we had called our older son, Josh, to come and pick up his little brother.

As soon as the doctor got started, I began screaming. It felt like he was pulling my tonsils out through my birthing canal. Lowell could hear me screaming from the waiting room, so he came racing back down the hall and into my room. The doctor instructed Lowell to lay on top of me to keep me on the table. I was screaming and trying to breathe deeply to relax at the same time.

I continued asking, "Why aren't we going to the operating room?"

With no shame or remorse, he told me that it was because he had a golfing engagement. Were I in OR and sedated, he would have to stay until I was recovered, causing him to miss his golf date.

I responded, "Why don't we trade places and see how you like it?"

When the procedure was finally completed, they brought Abe back to us wrapped in a tiny blanket. We cried as we held and kissed our infant son. I shared with the nurse that we were going to take Abe home. To my shock, I was told we couldn't. He was now considered the property of the hospital, and they needed to do tests on him. I was further told that the only lawful way I could get him out was by an undertaker. I was livid, and the mama bear in me resurrected. "There will be one here tomorrow morning. Get your nursing notes and quote me, 'If anything happens to this baby, I will sue all of you. I have never done this, I don't even believe in suing anyone, but I will if you destroy his body. He is as much our son as the rest of our boys.'"

I was absolutely furious. When they discharged me, I refused to walk out in my bloody clothes and told them to get me some paper scrubs. Lowell washed me up, helped me into the scrubs, and we headed home. I was broken, weeping for my son, but also crushed and angry because of the way I had been treated.

The next morning, I called the undertaker. He told me about a local Catholic hospital that had a miscarriage/stillborn ministry. They would even bury our son, free of charge, in a common grave, if that's what we wanted. He offered to transport Abe to the nearby Borgess Catholic Hospital to a nun by the name of Sister Susan.

When Sister Susan called me, I told her how I felt. She was very compassionate as well as informative. She said that while we decided what we wanted to do, she would keep Abe preserved in her office for up to a month. She told me it was of the utmost importance for my future mental well-being that I have peace about this situation.

After praying and seeking God, we decided to have Abe buried on top of my mother's grave, directly over her but only three feet down. We had a small service with our immediate family and the pastor. I finally had peace, and Abe's body was at rest.

PROPHECY / NOVEMBER 1995

Lowell and I went out of town one evening to hear an evangelist. We had never seen Burton Seavy before but had heard many wonderful things about his ministry. Arriving early, we found that a large crowd had already gathered, and expectations were high.

The service began with praise and worship, opening up our spirits to receive from God. After we were seated, Pastor Seavy pointed directly at me and told me to come forward. When I arrived at his side, he confirmed that we had never met and he knew nothing about me. He said that the Spirit of God instructed him to tell me that God has given me a new lease on life. It's not over; it's just the beginning.

He further stated that I had not tasted and drunk from the cup of life, but I had drunk from the cup of sorrows, heartaches, hurts, and much betrayal. "But the Lord says, 'I will never leave you or forsake you or betray you. I am not the giver of sorrow, but I am the Cup of Joy. When you take My cup and drink of it fully, you will experience joy inexpressible and full of glory. I have promised you joy in your spirit, that I will give you that joy. But you say, "Where Lord and how? For I carry a heavy load."'

Seavy continued, "The Lord says: 'Yes, and that's the mistake. You carried the heavy load. You see, I am the Burden Bearer. You have carried the load and then gotten on My back, kind of like on a donkey or a mule. I'm supposed to take that load. But you said, "I'll just get on You, Lord," and you got up there with the load.'

"So now the Lord says 'I'm carrying you and the load. But that's not the way I meant it to be. When you take that load and cast all your care upon Me as I told you to do, you will see the beginning of joy. Yes, joy! I did not say happiness, you'll have that in abundance also, but joy is something no one can explain. In the midst of darkness, howling winds and troubles, distresses, problems and cut-throat situations, and things of darkness—even in the midst of that—my children know joy. Have I not said it's a joy that nobody can give, and nobody can take it away? Since I am the one giving it to you, the devil can't take it away!

'I am giving you joy in the most trying moments; and then I'm going to turn you around and turn you loose. I have called you to minister, and you will walk on serpents and scorpions, you're going to tread on demons. I have given you a gift of discerning of spirits. That's in you. It's destruction time for these spirits. They will say, "Oh no! LaDonna is around!" and they will flee.' Are you ready to receive that new anointing? The angel of God that ministers with me has manifested himself to me." (Seavy, cassette tape, 10-21-95)

As Seavy laid hands on my shoulders and spoke those words over me, it was difficult for both of us to remain standing under the strong anointing. This took place in November, 1995.

It's been 25 years since that prophecy. I have to admit that I still struggle at times with carrying the burdens and the cares and trying to fix things. I wish I could say from that day forward, that I have always rolled my cares onto the Lord, but that's not been the case. It has been a growing process, and God knows my heart. I repent and go on, daily walking closer with Jesus. His grace and mercy cover me.

Lowell was sitting on the porch when Miss Dolly jumped onto his lap, wanting to be held.

UNIQUE AND UNEXPECTED

HESTER JONES

After receiving my RN license, one of my very first jobs was at a local nursing home. I was the charge nurse one evening when we had a new admit to the facility. She was an older lady who had suffered a brain stem stroke, paralyzing her from the neck down.

She could not talk, due to a trach, and was being fed through a gastro tube in her stomach. She was alert and oriented, I was told, but could only communicate by blinking her eyes. When I entered her room, I got busy with the admission's paperwork.

Suddenly something happened that I had never before experienced. Mercy and compassion flooded me, and I began weeping uncontrollably. I asked Hester if I could pray for her. She blinked over and over again; I knew that meant "Yes." I found myself lying partially on the bed with half of me on top of her, my arms wrapped around her middle. Weeping still, I began praying in the Spirit, crying out to God to have mercy for this woman. "Health and healing come, Father God, pour out your love and mercy, and heal her." I instructed Hester to continue thanking God for healing, and to also keep trying to move even if it was just her little toe. I explained that in continuing to thank God, her healing would increase.

That day on the way home, I asked God what I could do to encourage Hester. It came to me to take a cassette player and Bible tapes on healing into her room. She could listen to them with ear phones. I kept those tapes playing throughout my shifts. Hester became so special to me. Even after I transferred to another facility, I continued visiting her.

After several months, she started moving her toes. We were much encouraged! While I praised God, Hester blinked repeatedly. She continued making progress and was now in rehab. Slowly, one day at a time, she was being healed.

A year passed. Then one day, when I came to see her, I became alarmed because she was not in her room! What had happened to my dear friend? I was relieved when the staff told me that Hester had been moved to another facility because she had made such good progress! They also shared that her trachea and g-tube had been removed, and she was now eating on her own. I was thrilled!

I drove directly to the other facility and asked to see her. As I began walking down the long hallway, I could see her in her room. She was standing with the aid of leg braces! I started running toward her, and when she saw me, she opened her arms wide, and we embraced, praising God. It was the first time I had heard her voice.

She said, "Girl, I will never forget the day you prayed for me; something powerful happened on the inside of me! You gave me hope when I had no hope, and you gave me a reason to live."

I said, "Look at you standing, walking, and talking. It's a miracle!"

We could not stop hugging each other and praising God. Thank you, Jesus! I continued to see her off and on for a period of time, but then we lost contact with each another.

A few years later, while at a doctor's appointment, I noticed a woman pushing a man in a wheelchair through the parking lot. To my amazement, it was Hester! Her husband had suffered a stroke, and she was caring for him at home. She still wore a brace on one leg. That was the last time I actually saw her.

Years passed when, one day, Hester came to mind. I asked, "Father God, where is Hester? You know where she is and can reveal it to me." A few days later, I went to a revival meeting. At the mid-day break, another lady who was attending came over to me. She asked if I'd like to come to her home for lunch, explaining that she lived nearby.

While getting acquainted, we shared our faith stories, and I mentioned Hester Jones. To my surprise, this lady said, "I believe I knew her!" I was so excited! She told me that Hester had cared for her husband until he died, and then she lived in an adult foster care home. She had been active there and often told the story of how she was healed. She would share about a particular nurse who had prayed for her while she was at the nursing home, and something big had happened! God had shown her mercy, pouring out His love, and she had been healed.

My new friend also shared that she knew Hester to be a Christian who was strong in her faith. I asked her where Hester was currently living, and she informed me that Hester had changed residences recently—having gone home to Glory about six months before. My heart was awestruck at God's goodness and His answer to my prayer so many years ago.

Through the years, I have learned that the things we experience, good or bad, can be used by God to bring Him honor and glory, if we will allow Him to do so. The pain I suffered may not have been God's perfect will for my life; but as I yielded to Him, He turned it around and used it for good. There is no wasted time or hardship. He can use it all to tell others of His unfailing love and great mercy, often in the most unique and unexpected ways. When we trust God, we don't have to understand everything.

I learned that even without answers to why everything happened as it did, I could open myself up to God. He has done a mighty work within, transforming me from the inside out. He has brought out joy and peace, where there previously was none. I was given a new power and a new freedom.

When I look back at my life, I realize Father God has always put me in the right place at the right time. I can make that declaration even over my horrible childhood, because I am now convinced that He was there with me every single moment.

By His Spirit within us, He will lead and guide us. If we walk in the light as He is the light, we will have no occasion for stumbling; but if we do, He is there with open arms, to pick us up and place us back onto solid ground.

MISS DOLLY

I have come to know God's voice. He is my good shepherd. *"...his sheep follow him because they know his voice" (John 10:4 NIV).*

This was made clear to me in the most unusual way when I owned a goat I affectionately dubbed "Dolly." She was with us for a few years and became my pet. I named her Dolly in honor of my grandpa. He had owned many goats. And because I was a bald baby with huge blue eyes, Grandpa's nickname for me had been "Dolly." He would often tell me that I looked just like a rubber dolly.

Miss Dolly routinely followed me on walks. If she saw me walking down the lane without her, she would call to me, bleating again and again. My father-in-law, upon seeing me running with Dolly beside me, would declare, "Here come the two old goats!" It got to be a family joke.

When Lowell and I decided that we would like to travel more, I gave Miss Dolly to our Amish friend, Nathaniel. He wanted to breed her and said I could have her milk for free.

One day, after not seeing Dolly for some time, I decided to find out how she was doing. When I arrived at Nathaniel's place, he told me that I would find Dolly out in the barn with the rest of the goats. He also informed me that she was pregnant; he thought she might be carrying twins.

I went to the barn and looked in, it was wall-to-wall goats everywhere. There seemed to be a hundred goats, and they all looked alike to me. I couldn't find Dolly, because I couldn't tell which goat was her. So I yelled, "Miss Dolly! Where are you?" In fear, all the goats scattered and ran away, except one. Miss Dolly, still knowing my voice, ran right to me! But to the rest I was a stranger, making them fearful.

I was amazed, and immediately the scripture about God's sheep knowing His voice came to mind, especially the line that says, *"But they will never follow a stranger; in fact, they will run away from him because they do not recognize a stranger's voice"*

(John 10:5 NIV). Because I had spent lots of time with Dolly, she remembered my voice.

When she came to me, I loved on her and could tell that she was happy to see me too. I said, "Why, look at you, you're as big as a barrel!" Somehow I knew she was not having twins but triplets. A few weeks later, she did birth triplets, but unfortunately, got mastitis and died. It was a very sad day for me, having to say goodbye to my dear Dolly.

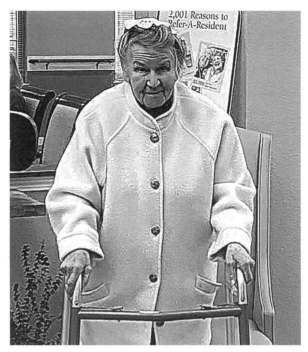

My dear friend, Verna, still bears
fruit in her old age, proclaiming
the word of the Lord.

BEAUTIFUL FEET

God sent a godly woman into my life who stands out among many. Verna is a 92-year-old woman of faith who I learned to know through our church. She resides in an adult foster care home, prays regularly for the other residents there, and preaches the Word to them. She is an encouragement to all who get to know her. Every time I visit with her, I feel like I'm soaking up faith. We share testimonies with each other as well as praise reports. Her life has not been easy, having experienced many struggles herself. But she chose to serve God, and she still does. She has shared with me many stories about God's faithfulness.

After my visits with Verna, I always come away enriched, built up, edified, and encouraged. Because she prays the Word of God, her prayers are powerful and dynamic. At the end of our latest visit and prayer time, I knelt down in front of her to put her socks and shoes on. Before I left, I thanked her for blessing me.

Early the following morning at 4:30, I woke up and "saw" Verna's feet, like a vision. A Bible verse came to my mind: *"...How beautiful are the feet of those who bring good news" (Romans 10:15 NIV)!* Then I "heard" her voice praying, and I recalled the words she had prayed over me the previous day. Tears flowed as I recognized how deeply she had touched my heart. I was still receiving from the words she had spoken over me. At 92 years of age, she is truly a godly example and still ministers to the body of Christ.

FAITH COACH

Over the years, God has been faithful to send mentors to teach and assist me in my walk of faith. One was a gentleman I never actually met in person. We had mutual Christian friends and communicated on social media. Some people have an exercise coach or life coach. I thought of Edgar as a faith coach. He had an anointing to evangelize, often leading people to the Lord.

He told me his faith stories and adventures while doing street ministry where he led thousands to Jesus! He frequently gave them Bibles and prayed for them. Edgar challenged me to live for Jesus in an even greater measure. I would ask questions, and he would tell me how to draw nearer to God and how to hear His voice clearly. He taught me how to really read the Word of God and about the importance of kneeling to pray early in the morning. He said if I would humble myself, God would use me.

He also taught me to prepare my heart to share Jesus with others every day, looking for open doors, and being bold. "Let the Spirit of God lead you. You must be thick-skinned and not easily offended. If people reject you, you just love them," he said. He also inspired me to pray daily in my prayer language for the perfect will of God.

God had sent him to coach me. And just as God had sent him, one day we both knew his work with me was done. Edgar had completed what God assigned him to do.

Everyone needs someone to mentor them, train them, and model godliness. Edgar was like Paul, who said, *"Follow my example, as I follow the example of Christ" (1 Corinthians 11:1 NIV)*. As my brother in Christ, Edgar had a great influence on me, building me up in God's Word. He was truly a man of prayer. Many profited from his godly example and teachings,

Edgar, sharing the love of Jesus
on the streets

including those who received his wisdom second-hand through me.

GIFTS AND CALLINGS

During one of my early morning prayer times, seeking Father God and interceding, I had a vision. I was on the floor, face down, and had already prayed for over an hour in the Spirit. In my mind, I saw a tall glass vase sitting on a table. The thought came to me that it was a vessel.

The vase was filled with many balls of different colors: red, blue, green, purple, and white. A bright light shone on the vase. It turned slowly with each ball changing color as the light illuminated them, one by one. Father God spoke to my heart. "I have placed many gifts and callings within you. As my light shines on you, they will come to the surface and shine." *"Let your light so shine before men, that they may see your good works and glorify your Father in heaven" (Matthew 5:16).*

I somehow knew that every color of each ball represented a different gift and calling. It was the light of God's love and anointing that brought forth the gift and calling from within the vessel. I felt greatly loved and wept with joy.

We are all vessels for His honor and glory. He places different gifts and callings within each of us and then uses us to touch others. It's His anointing that makes the difference. *"Most assuredly, I say to you, he who believes in Me, the works that I do he will do also, and greater works than these he will do, because I go to My Father" (John 14:12).*

IT'S NOT ABOUT YOU

I believe my nursing profession was an avenue where God used me to serve others and to share His Word. My assignment was to encourage people and stir them up to serve Him. Someone once told me that I was an igniter, lighting a fire on the inside of people.

Over the years, I worked in many different areas of nursing, but my beginning was in a nursing home, where I discovered that I loved elderly people. I observed that they were never esteemed highly enough. I learned much from many of those residents and had countless opportunities to love them with the Love of God.

One of our residents was an elderly lady who was dying. She lingered for many days, not eating or drinking. It was surprising to all of us that she was still alive. One day, after getting her report, I asked the staff, "Why is she still here? Is there someone she is waiting for?"

They said, "Yes, she has a son who lives two blocks away, but he won't come and see his mother."

I said, "Well, he will when I get done with him!" I called her son and said, "This is LaDonna, the charge nurse; I'm calling to inform you that your mother is dying and you need to come see her." He was silent for a few moments, then told me that he wanted to remember his mother the way she had been, and not to see her so sick.

I said, "Sir, pardon me, but this is not about you, this is about your mama who needs to see her only child before she dies."

Again there was silence. Then he quietly said, "I'm actually afraid."

"Of course you are, but I will go with you." I told him he would be better able to handle the grieving process, when it was all over, by coming to see his mother and making peace. He said he would be there shortly.

He approached the nurses' station a few minutes later, and I went with him to his mother's room. Lowering the railing on her bed, I pulled up a chair and told him to sit down. Then I took his mother's hand and placed it in his hand. I said, "Repeat after me, 'Mom I love you; you were the best mom ever.'"

He began to weep, asking, "Can I have a few minutes alone with my mom?"

Sometimes, we have to "prime the pump," as I call it, to get them started. Then they will pick up their responsibility and get on with it.

"Of course you can, and take as long as you need."

About half an hour later, he came out of her room, looking like a wreck. I could see that he had been sobbing. He thanked me for insisting that he come to tell his mother goodbye. His visit had given him closure. I asked if I should call him when she passed. Hesitantly, he asked if he would have to come back. I said, "No, it's not necessary." When he left, I went down to her room to check on her and to put the rail back in place. His mama had already passed. I called his home, and his wife informed me that he was just pulling into the driveway. I told her to please tell her husband that his mama had passed in peace after telling her only son goodbye.

MITTEN MONEY

Ben, our youngest, was ready to begin school. At the encouragement of a teacher friend, I decided to homeschool him. I had already discovered that Ben was an easy learner, having taught him to read at four years of age. So I continued to work part-time, second shift, and homeschooled him in the mornings. Lowell was then with him while I worked.

Although it was a sacrifice, we managed. I actually found it very rewarding.

I enrolled Ben in a homeschool group, along with playing sports: swimming, baseball, golf, and basketball. He was also in 4-H. All of those activities gave Ben lots of healthy interaction with other children. We had him tested yearly to make sure that he was meeting public school standards. Extra activities included Bible quizzing and memorization to compete on a Bible knowledge team, guitar lessons, and playing guitar at church.

Ben then went on to college. He ended up taking college courses online through College Plus, earning a bachelor's degree in International Business.

For twelve years, I worked and homeschooled simultaneously. Many years before attempting homeschooling, I had said that I would have become a teacher, had I not decided on nursing. As it turned out, I ended up doing both!

When Ben was about 17, he decided to do a one-year internship through our church. The cost was $3000, but Ben had no time for additional work outside of his current cleaning duties at the church. Because the amount needed was beyond our regular budget, I asked God how I could help cover this expense. God's answer came quickly, "Use what you have."

I thought, "What do I have that could earn $3000?" Then I remembered that a friend had given me a pattern to sew mittens cut from recycled wool sweaters. I had already made some for Christmas gifts and still had some extra pairs left. Maybe I could sell them.

I prayed about how much I should charge, considering how much I had invested in them and how much time they took me to make. I then consulted with friends and family, asking what they considered a fair price. I didn't want to overcharge, but I wanted to make them financially affordable to everyone.

After finally settling on $20 a pair, I had an opportunity to take the mittens I had on hand to a nearby craft show. All 17 pairs sold, and a local merchant asked to put some in his store! Greatly anticipating this opportunity, I asked my daughter-in-law, Candi, to make some business cards for me using the Scripture, *"She seeks wool and flax, and willingly works with her hands" (Proverbs 31:13).*

I sewed my miracle mittens
from recycled wool sweaters.

I started sewing like crazy! I also got the idea of finding a basket at Goodwill and filling it with several pairs of mittens. I carried that basket with me everywhere I went, peddling mittens in every unit of the hospital and even at the bank. Friends and family supported my endeavor. They sold so fast that I knew it was supernatural.

I started a bank account, naming it "Mitten Money." People usually bought more than one pair, giving the extras away as gifts. I also felt prompted to give away many pairs myself, at no cost, to those I knew couldn't afford them. I was amazed to see how rapidly my new enterprise took off.

My business did so well I had to hire my sister-in-law, Linda, to help with the sewing. I shared with people why I was making mittens, as well as the story of how I had gotten my business idea by praying.

Not only did I pay for the bulk of Ben's internship but also covered Ben's trip to Israel with a church group and our pastor. I continued to praise God and share my story. And I still had mitten money left! It seemed to me that it was holy money, and I refused to spend it on myself. So I started giving funds to each of the other interns to help with their expenses. It was nothing short of a miracle!

During that time, I sewed more than three hundred pairs of mittens! *"And my God shall supply all your need according to His riches in glory by Christ Jesus" (Philippians 4:19). "Fear the Lord, you his holy people, for those who fear him lack nothing" (Psalm 34:9 NIV).*

LISTENING WITH MY HEART

One day while I was sewing mittens in the basement, I heard a knock at the front door. I was sure it was the Schwan's man selling ice cream and other products. I was busy and really didn't want to stop sewing, but I felt like I should. Sure enough, it was the Schwan's man. As I was looking through his catalog of products, I noticed he was yawning a lot. When he went to collect my food items from his truck, the Lord spoke to my heart, "I want you to pray for him."

I said, "Father God, we are talking about the Schwan's man. I don't even know him." But I knew that I must be obedient, or I'd miss God's leading.

So when he returned, I said, "I really don't know you well, and don't even know if you're a Christian, but while you were out at your truck, God spoke to my heart and told me to pray for you."

He burst into tears and began shaking all over. I told him to sit down and tell me what was going on. He had just found out that his wife was having an affair. Although she had repented and asked for forgiveness, he could not stop thinking about it or forgive her. He was tormented to the point of not being able to sleep.

Before he arrived at my door, he had asked God to help him and to send someone to pray for him. I was his very next stop. Thank God I was obedient! I prayed for him, ministered to him, and counseled with him, giving him my phone number in case he and his wife needed help. I continued covering them in prayer as God brought them to mind, asking Him to meet his need and to restore their relationship. It's been many years since then, and they are still together, their marriage healed and restored by our Mighty God.

My nursing career was greatly used by God.
I worked in several different areas of nursing
and went on two medical mission trips.

NURSING STORIES

WORKING IN ICU

I eventually moved to the hospital for my employment, working Rehab for about six months before moving into ICU. There too, I had lots of opportunities to pray with people and witness to them.

Suddenly one day, the doors to ICU flew open, and an Acute Care patient was rushed in on his hospital bed. He was in flash pulmonary edema and having difficulty breathing—a genuine emergency. I quickly assessed the situation and, without delay, began hooking him up to the monitor. The doctor was yelling orders at me to give him IV medications to stabilize him, followed by one demand after another. I could see from the monitor what the patient's vital signs were and his heart rhythm; I knew we were losing him. He was "circling the drain," as we called it. My heart was racing. We were doing everything we knew to do but to no avail. The patient was wide-eyed and fearful, sitting straight up in bed and trying to breathe. Suddenly, I found myself yelling at the man, "Repent! You're going to split hell wide open if you don't!"

Obviously, this was a very tense and awkward moment. But he was going to die, and out of the abundance of God's truth in my heart, and by His prompting, I had spoken. The patient began crying and repenting of his sins as fast as he could, asking for forgiveness and mercy. The monitor pattern leveled out, returning to a normal sinus rhythm, and he lived. The doctor looked at me strangely. I just shrugged my shoulders. "It worked." I wondered later if my yelling prompted a supernatural electrical shock to his heart by the Spirit of God, putting it back into a normal sinus rhythm.

I worked in ICU for ten years and spoke to countless nurses, therapists, patients, and doctors about the love of God. I just shared testimonies from my heart, letting God do the rest. Years later, a few nurses came back to tell me, "I know you thought I wasn't listening, but I was, and your words meant a lot to me."

Another ICU experience happened as I was taking care of a man who kept saying that the devils and demons had come to take him to hell. He would swing his arms in the air, duck his head, and insist that they were biting him. He was on no meds or drugs and was alert and oriented otherwise. Since he was my only patient at the time, I went to his bedside and spoke with him about the love of God. He told me that he had once painted a Catholic Church but had never attended one.

I told him that God had a plan and purpose for him and loved him, and that he did not have to go to hell. God came to seek and save those who are lost and sent his son, Jesus, to die for his sin. He said salvation was impossible for him because of all the horrible things he had done. I assured him it didn't matter, because God's mercy and forgiveness were far greater and were always available to him. Then I shared several Scripture verses with him.

He insisted again, "No, I can't be saved."

I went into the break room to pray, asking God to open his heart to receive salvation. I continued to intercede for him. I went to him a second time and shared about God's love and mercy. He listened again but to no avail.

At the end of my shift, I told him that even though I was going home, he could still ask God to forgive him and accept Jesus into his heart without me there. He assured me he understood and would think about it.

Returning to work the next day, I asked the respiratory therapist what had happened to the patient in bed three. He told me it was terrible, the worst thing he'd ever seen. An emergency code had been called because the man was screaming and crying out in agony, still convinced that the devils and demons were taking him to hell. Like the previous day, he was still swinging his arms back and forth and claiming they were biting him. There was nothing they could do to save him, and he died. The respiratory therapist was really shaken by the whole experience.

I said, "Well, there's nothing we can do for him now. But what about you, do you know Jesus?"

He stood up, "I don't want to talk about this," and he walked out of the room.

HOMECARE AND HOSPICE

In 2010, I transferred to Homecare and Hospice and soon realized that was my passion—where my heart was. Led by the Holy Spirit, I was able to pray with my patients and speak freely in their homes. Some kept my phone number for many years, calling me to pray with them or to ask for advice. The majority of my patients at first were simply that—patients. But as I attended to each of them with empathy and respect, giving the best care possible, we became friends. And before I knew it, I was family to them. My gift from God, of mercy and compassion, empowered me to truly love them and connect with them. He gave me a servant's heart, and I found that serving my patients was truly fulfilling as well as rewarding. Because of my countless opportunities to speak life to my patients, many of my "Jesus stories" come from that time period.

FLASH BACK FROM THE PAST

Recently, I was sent by Homecare to see an elderly lady I had never seen before. She had sores on her lower legs. As I was applying lotion to her legs, she told me she was 80 years old and had stood many hours on those legs. She went on to tell me that she used to be a beautician. When I asked where, much to my amazement, it had been in my hometown. She said one particular thing had troubled her for years, and she still felt just awful about it.

I asked, "What might that be?"

She went on to tell me about a woman who had called many years ago to make an appointment for her daughter to get a haircut. When she arrived with her little girl, the child had long flowing hair down her back and seemed totally unaware that it would soon be cut. When the girl realized what was about to happen, she cried, begging her mom not to cut it off, because she loved her long hair. But the mother insisted it be cut, and so it was. She had felt so bad for the young girl and thought she probably still hated her.

She went on to say that the girl's last name was Bingaman, my maiden name! I knew instantly that she was talking about my little sister, Shirley, and told her so. She was both shocked and amazed. I explained that my sister had cried every time Mom had brushed her long hair. She had been warned again and again that Mother was going to get it cut off if she didn't stop crying.

When I returned home, I called my sister for verification. My sister clearly remembered the incident, the shop, and its location. My sister, now 62 years old, assured me that she had forgiven the beautician long ago and held no bitterness towards her. I shared Shirley's words on my next visit with that patient. She was greatly relieved! We marveled at how Father God had led me to her, intentionally crossing our paths, to bring her peace.

PRAYERS FOR JASON

I recognized early on that doing hospice was definitely God's call on my life. My patients impacted me greatly, touching me at the center of my being.

Jason, in his late 30's, was another one of my patients. He was my youngest patient to die in hospice. He had lung cancer. His mother and brother had both lost their battles with cancer the previous year, and now Jason was battling for his life. He was a quiet, reserved man who loved the outdoors, the woods, fishing, and hunting.

During my weekly assessments at his home, I would try to penetrate the wall he had built up on the inside. He would sit and watch TV, zoning me out. I would prattle on and on, asking him questions and hoping to get him to interact. He did not want to talk to me or anyone else. There was obviously an inner struggle going on, and he was determined not to talk about it. After several attempts over the weeks, I decided I was going to back off, letting God deal directly with him. I prayed that God would open his heart and allow me to help him.

Then one day, Jason actually spoke. He told me that he thought maybe the tumor had shrunk and that he'd like to go back to the oncologist for an MRI. I told him that was fine and asked him to sign the necessary paperwork, revoking hospice, in order to seek out his doctor and the procedure that he wanted. I desperately hoped he was correct and told him I would stay in touch. If he ever needed me, I would come back.

A few days after the MRI was completed, I called Jason's home to learn the outcome. His wife told me it was not good. The MRI had actually shown that the cancer was spreading. Jason was so depressed that he refused to get out of bed. In fact, he was currently at home, lying in a fetal position, crying. "I will be right there. Tell Jason to get up because I'm coming over, not as his nurse but as his friend."

When I arrived, he had just gotten out of bed and was walking into the dining room. I told him to sit down, that we were going to have a Come-to-Jesus talk. Then I laid out the plan of salvation, telling him that God has always loved him. "He is for you, not against you. The doctors have done all they can, so your only hope for real life is in Jesus. He is the healer of our spirits, our souls, and our bodies. God gave up His Son to die so you can live! What is it going to be—abundant life or death? There is more to this life than what we see, hear, and feel here on earth. God deeply loves you."

He leaned over the table weeping, and reaching his hand out to me, asked, "Will you pray for me to know Jesus?"

I answered, "It would be my honor and privilege to introduce you to my closest friend and God." I turned to look at his wife standing near us, "Do you want in on this too?"

She simply responded, "Yes." We joined hands and prayed the prayer of salvation; they both received Jesus as their Lord and Savior!

Jason went back on hospice. It was only a few short weeks before he went into a coma and became unresponsive. One evening, his wife called me, crying, to tell me Jason was gone. She shared that she had been at his bedside holding his hand for hours with no response from him—not one word. Suddenly, his eyes flew open wide, and he looked up. He was smiling really big like he saw something, maybe an angel or a loved one or a glimpse of heaven. Then he looked at her, nodded, and took his last breath. Jason was home free.

AMISH HERITAGE

I have acquired many Amish friends over the years that I have come to love and appreciate. My mother's Amish heritage may have had something to do with that. I love their unique, simple lifestyle and hard work ethic and have had many opportunities to share and fellowship with them. They return my love with appreciation, admiration, and respect. I have attended their weddings and funerals. Some have been my patients in Homecare and Hospice.

Orpha, an Amish woman, called one day to say that her mom was not doing well. She explained that the doctor and nurse were currently too busy with patients at their office to come for a home visit. She asked if I would come. We had previously

My mother in law with me dressed up as an
Amish woman for a harvest party

My maternal grandparents—Jacob
and Anna Beachy—of Arthur, Illinois

discussed her mother's health problems, as well as the dying process.

I drove to her home and quickly noted that the situation was serious. Several buggies were already parked in the yard. The Amish are very supportive of one another, especially family. As I entered the home, I saw several family members weeping and praying. The mother, looking lethargic, was seated near a window, using an oxygen tank that had been borrowed from a neighbor. I was asked to assess her condition, so I took her vital signs and listened to her heart and lungs. It was obvious to me that she was dying. She told me that she did not want to go to the hospital, that she was at peace and eager to get to heaven. I told the others that I expected her to pass soon.

"What should we do?" they asked.

I replied, "You're already doing it. I can't think of a better way to die than with family and friends gathered around me."

They formed a circle and began to sing in German. It was absolutely beautiful, almost angelic! After singing, the oldest daughter, who was the caregiver, stepped forward and spoke quietly to her mother. "It's okay to go home to be with Jesus." She assured her that they would all be fine, even though they would miss her, and that they loved her very much. Stepping back into the circle, the daughter then nodded at me. I went over to her mother and assessed her for the last time. "She has passed and is now home, free with her Heavenly Father."

They looked bewildered about what to do next. I assured them that I would handle everything. I pronounced her and documented the time, called her physician and the undertaker with a report, and made the necessary arrangements.

I suggested that the women move their loved one to the bed, bathe her, and change her clothes. I explained that it would be the last loving thing they could do for her. The children, who were soon due home from school, could view her before she was taken to the funeral home. The Amish build their own coffins.

The funeral service would be held in a few days inside a pole barn, where church services were normally conducted. I knew many would come to show their respect and to comfort the family. I was invited also.

When I arrived at the funeral, I asked the usher in charge where the "English section" was. He inquired if I was family or a friend, and would I be content to sit where he told me. I replied, "Yes, I do not want to be out of order. I am the RN who was there when she passed."

At that he left me and went to speak with the family. He soon returned and asked me to follow him. I was ushered right to the front, where there were four chairs facing the crowd: three for the pastors on one side of the coffin and one for me on the other side. I was being seated in the place of honor, and I was humbled. I was also thankful that I had chosen to wear my long, black, woolen coat because it reached to my ankles.

After the service, a son of the deceased approached me and offered to pay me for my services. I refused, explaining that that was not my motive for helping. He proceeded to tell me that I was one of the few English who treated them with respect, didn't belittle them, or think they were ignorant. I assured him that I would never treat them that way, and that his people were my people, coming as I did from Amish roots.

I drove all the elderly grandmas to the gravesite in my Suburban. It was winter and bitter cold. I loved watching how they buried their dear sister. They sang hymns and then passed a shovel around. Everyone shoveled dirt into the grave. It was a beautiful experience and touched my heart deeply. I hope, when my time comes, that I will be buried in the same way. What an honor and privilege to serve those from my heritage! I know my mother would be pleased.

HOW GOD SEES US

One of my patients, Mary, remarked one day about the strangeness of some Christians. She had been watching a TV program when I arrived. I went about setting up my computer and doing a start-of-care admission. I had never met Mary before, but she continued talking about this program and directing questions to me.

I finally responded to her, "It's like this, there are many people who know all about God, but they don't have a personal relationship with Him. They can quote scriptures and say they are Christians, but they have no fruit in their lives. Take us, for example. I may know your social security number, your address, your insurance carrier, your medical history, and even what meds you take. But if you asked if I know you, the answer is "No. While I know all about you, I don't really have a relationship with you."

She inquired, "Where did you learn that?"

I told her it was hot off the press, that the Holy Spirit just revealed it to me.

She said, "I want what you have in my life." I then had the privilege of praying with her and leading her to Jesus.

The angel of the Lord encamps all around those who fear Him, and delivers them. *Psalm 34:7*

Christmas gift from Omar (artist) and family. God gave them this vision.

14
GLORY STORIES

I recall the day I went to a woman's home to do a start-of-care. Her house was filthy dirty and full of stuff. I could tell that this patient was a hoarder. She also kept about 20 cats in her house, so the smell was overpowering. There was only a narrow path between all the piles of stuff. After completing all the needed paperwork, I left her house, went to my car, and thoroughly sprayed myself with air freshener.

I considered assigning this patient to someone else. But instantly, Father God reminded me about the promise I had made to Him, that I would allow Him to bring me the patients He wanted me to have. So I kept her.

As I planned each day's schedule of patients, I always made her my last stop. I didn't want to offend my other patients with the foul odor I carried after being at Debbie's house. During the time she was my patient, I started each morning by praying for her, that Father God would prepare her heart and give me opportunities to share the love of Jesus.

After a few weeks of caring for her, while I was changing her dressing, she commented that I looked tired. I said, "Yes, I was up at 4:30 a.m." She asked why I would ever get up that early. I thought, "Well here is my open door." I answered, "To pray for you and the rest of my patients."

She was shocked, wondering why I would pray for her. I asked her if she was a Christian and she said no, adding that she really didn't know much about Christianity, nor understand it. I proceeded to tell her that Jesus loves her and that God has had a plan and purpose for her life ever since she was in her mother's womb. She told me no one has ever loved her and that she has no friends. She shared that as a little girl, she had stayed in the barn with the animals most of the time. They were her friends and did not condemn her or make fun of her but accepted her as she was. It struck me then why she owned so many cats; they were her friends! Mercy and compassion rose up in me, and I told her more about the love of God. It was difficult for her to think that anyone could love her.

I offered to pray with her. Because she was receptive, I got on my knees, and we both wept as I led her into a relationship with the Lord. She immediately wanted to pray for me! She thanked God for sending me to tell her the truth about His love for her and that He now accepted her as His own daughter.

Everyone needs the love of God, along with His mercy and forgiveness. Sometimes we see only the surface of a person, as I had initially with Debbie. There was far more going on within her, and God revealed it to me as she told about her past.

GOD PROVIDES SHOES

As a Homecare and Hospice nurse, I have met many lovely people, like the elderly couple, Fred and Laura. Years before, they had crashed their airplane. God had miraculously saved them, restoring them to health, even though both had been badly burned and carried many scars on their bodies. I enjoyed them so much that I scheduled them as my last patients of the day so we could spend extra time together. I often shared my faith stories with them.

One day Laura said, "Let's have a cup of tea and you can tell us one of your faith stories. We love to hear what God is doing."

I thought for a moment, praying silently about what I should share. It came to me to tell them about a young man from our church that had some financial needs. I was hesitant because I don't usually tell anyone when we bless others financially. The prompting was persistent, so I knew this was the story I was to share.

We asked our son, Ben, to talk to the young man to find out his needs. He told Ben he badly needed a new pair of shoes for church, although he wasn't sure what size he wore, maybe 12 or 12½. So I planned to give him money to purchase new shoes.

In the meantime, I was at a secondhand store looking for clothes for myself. The thought kept coming to me to go look at the shoe rack. I ignored that thought several times. I didn't need shoes. But then I decided to wander over to the shoe rack and at least take a look. Just as I thought, they were all well-worn. But as I turned to leave, I spotted a pair of men's shoes on the bottom row. They were size 12½, made in the USA of black leather, and appeared to be in very good condition! I checked the soles and also ran my hand over the insoles. Why, they looked like they had never been worn! So I bought them for $10, thinking I could always bring them back. Amazingly, they were a perfect fit for the young man at church. He told us that they were the nicest shoes he'd ever owned.

While relaying this story, I had noticed Fred and Laura exchanging frequent glances. So as I finished the story, I asked them "What's up?"

Laura blurted out, "Those were Fred's shoes! He had worn them only once to church."

Fred said, "They cost $98."

I was shocked and asked, "So why did you get rid of them?"

"Well," Fred proceeded to explain, "my feet got swollen, and my shoes were always too tight, so I bought a larger pair of shoes. But after I bought them, the swelling went away, making them too big. We kept them for several months just in case I needed them, but my feet didn't swell up again. Since it was too late to return the shoes, we decided to donate them. We prayed that someone who really needed them would get them."

I felt prompted by the Holy Spirit to use this to reassure them of how valuable they were to God, even in their advanced years. I said, "Here you were, thinking you were of no value and wondering how God could possibly use you for His kingdom. But God did use you to minister to someone who had a need. You blessed a young man with a nice pair of shoes. You're never too old. God will use you for His honor and glory if you are willing and obedient."

Both had tears in their eyes and were blessed to know that they, too, had been a blessing to someone else.

(This story appeared in Guideposts magazine in May/June, 2013)

DORMANT SEEDS

It was 1983. My mother, two of my sons, and I took a trip to Texas. We planned to stay a week and visit family. My sister, Shirley, lived in a duplex and next door to her lived her brother-in-law, Pat, and his friend, Kenny. I had never met Pat or Kenny, but it didn't take us long to get acquainted. My sons wanted to play games at Pat's place with cousins, but I was protective and didn't want them unattended. Almost daily we hung out at Pat and Kenny's place, talking and getting to know each other.

Shirley's brother-in-law, Pat

After some time, they confessed that they had been warned about me—that I was a religious nut who talked a lot about God. I replied that I indeed was a Christian with a personal relationship with Jesus Christ, if that's what they meant. We discussed the Word of God, and I shared my testimony about God's hand in my life, along with many faith-filled stories. They began asking many questions.

During that week, I prayed a lot for Pat and Kenny. But too soon we were scheduled to leave. I assured them that although I was leaving, Father God would never leave them or forsake them, and that the Holy Spirit would lead and guide them.

Both Pat and Kenny had received Jesus into their hearts previously. I bought them each a new reader-friendly Bible and encouraged them to read it. I also contacted local Bible-believing churches and instructed them to attend one. I left, went home and never heard from them again.

Recently, 38 years later, Shirley contacted me and told me Pat had been diagnosed with lung cancer. I was grieved to hear it and began praying for him. I felt in my heart that I needed to see him. To my amazement Shirley informed me that he currently lived in Michigan near me. She gave me his phone number and address and I contacted him. Yes, he wanted to see me.

I had difficulty finding his location, so I finally pulled over and prayed in the spirit for wisdom. I then drove right to his home. I knocked, and he slowly opened the door. He looked emaciated, tired, weak, and older than his years. We sat on the porch and talked while he smoked a cigarette.

When he was diagnosed with cancer, he hit rock bottom. However, he said, "I never forgot the Word of God you shared with me all those years ago. My eyes were opened, my heart received forgiveness, and Jesus came to me. I believe this cancer was my wake-up call. I'm thankful for God's mercy and compassion in giving me another chance. I now read my Bible daily, and it gives me peace."

It had been 38 years, and we both marveled at the love of God and how far it reached. He said repeatedly, "I'm at peace and ready to go home." I offered to pray for healing for him, but he refused. "I know it's my time. Do you think God still loves me even though I still smoke?"

"Pat," I said, "nothing can stop the love of God. We have all sinned and fallen short of the glory of God. Your spirit is willing but your flesh is weak. Smoking will not keep you out of heaven, but it does not glorify God."

Our meeting was cut short when Pat had to lie down. He was tired, weak, and in pain. He again thanked me for sharing the love of God with him years ago. Then I prayed with him.

A week later he called me with a question. "When I'm in bed, I see people in long white robes walking around me." I asked how that made him feel. "Very peaceful," he answered. I told him I believed they were angels. He responded, "Just as I thought, I knew you would tell me the truth and that you would know." A few days later, Pat called again and said that today he was leaving. He thanked me again, adding that he loved me for sharing Jesus with him.

The seed had been sown many years prior, and because life was in the seed, it sprouted forth. It did not die but lay dormant until it was nurtured and watered, producing eternal life. God's Word is powerful, active, and alive and bears fruit in our lives.

HIGHEST COMPLIMENT

Then there was Tommy. He had a rare lung disease. His wife had cared for him for 21 years, and now he was on hospice. His journey was coming to a close. I soon felt close to Tommy and Caryn, counting them as dear friends, and they treated me like family. Often when people share a life-changing event, a strong bond is created that changes the relationship from acquaintance to deep friendship.

Caryn and I have remained friends over the years. Tommy and Caryn once gave me the highest compliment I have ever received—"When you come, peace comes." My greatest desire is to be a carrier of Jesus, to be a vessel of His peace, love, hope and joy to the world.

EARLY MORNING PRAYER

A few years ago, my cousin, Marg, offered us her winter home in Florida for a two-week vacation—a very generous offer. Lowell and I agreed it would be nice to get out of the winter weather, so we decided to take her up on her offer. "When you're ready to go, just let me know, and I'll get you the keys," Marg promised.

As our vacation time approached, I told Lowell I was unsure about going to Florida and that we should pray about where God wanted us to go. So we set ourselves in agreement, asking for God's wisdom and direction as to where we should go on vacation.

Within just a few days, Lowell asked, "What about San Antonio, Texas, to see my uncle and aunt, Sam and Adeline Graber?"

Instantly in my heart, I knew this was exactly where we were supposed to go. We made plans, and our Texas relatives were excited to hear we were coming.

In the meantime, as part of my regular routine, I got up early to pray. Before I had even left my bedroom, the Spirit of God spoke to my heart, "Pray for Katurah."

I thought, "Who is Katurah?" The only Katurah I knew worked for KCI, a wound vac company, and I ordered supplies for my patients through her. For whatever reason, I thought her company was located in Grand Rapids, Michigan. Because I did not personally know her or her needs, I prayed in the Spirit for Katurah. This continued for several days.

After a week or so of interceding for her, I called Katurah to order more wound vacuum supplies. Once the order was placed, I asked her if I could speak to her on a more personal level when she had time.

"I have time now, actually," she replied.

"Although I don't know you personally," I began, "I would like to share with you that I am a Christian, and I get up early every morning to pray. Several days ago, God spoke to my heart to pray for you over the Christmas holiday. I want you to know that I have been praying and interceding for you."

She burst into tears and said, "I can't talk to you right now," and hung up.

I didn't know what to think. Did I offend her, or did I hit a tender spot in her heart?

I rolled my cares onto the Lord, remaining confident in what He had spoken to my heart about praying for her.

A couple weeks later, I called KCI to order extra supplies. I didn't want the nurses who were covering for me to run out of supplies while I was in Texas. After I had submitted my order, Katurah wondered why I was reordering so soon. I explained about my vacation and wanting to be sure that the nursing staff had plenty while I was gone.

She asked, "Where are you going?"

"San Antonio, Texas," I answered.

Before I could say anything more, she exclaimed, "You're coming to see me?"

I was more than surprised, especially since I thought KCI was in Michigan. But no, of course it was located in San Antonio, right where God was sending us!

Katurah explained that she had lost a son to cancer a few years back, and now the holidays were very painful without him. She thanked me for praying, confessing that when I had previously told her about God instructing me to pray for her, she'd been overcome by His love, mercy, and compassion. That's why she had ended the call so quickly.

Wanting to see me, Katurah asked when I would be in San Antonio. My steps were certainly ordered by the Lord. He had known her need all along. We did meet up, and she shared her story as she wept. Although she had two other sons, she was still fighting grief and sorrow. I shared God's love with her and prayed with her. Then I gave her a Bible and several Christian books I had purchased and brought with me, knowing they would minister to her and help promote the healing of her broken heart. When we are willing and obedient, God will send us across the country to minister, even just to one person.

PROPHECY GIVEN

While we were in Texas, my sister, Shirley, and I attended a prayer meeting at Fountain Gate Church. We went to pray, seek God, and worship. We were told about two women who would prophesy over people if they so desired. I signed up and was called to a back room. I told them nothing about myself, except that I was from Michigan, visiting my sister, and had attended their Sunday service for my first time with her.

They began to pray in the Spirit, holding my hand. Then they told me that my husband adored me, repeating it three times. They prophesied that God had called me to be an igniter to set people on fire for Him. I would stir people up to serve God in a greater measure, and I was to seek Him. One of the ladies said, "I see you praying for hundreds of

With Katurah

dark-skinned people. I see them lined up as far as the eye can see." She added that God would use me to minister to them. She asked me if any of this bore witness within me or meant anything to me.

I said, "No, but I'm going to hold it in my heart, set it up on a spiritual shelf, and wait on Father God to show me. I will not disregard it."

A few days later, we left Texas and began driving home to Michigan. Along the way, we stopped in Illinois to see my cousin, Theresa. While we were there, we joined her family at their church and enjoyed a sermon and a good time of fellowship. As we were leaving, the pastor stopped us, asking Theresa to introduce me, which she did. He said he doesn't normally do this, but the Lord had given him a prophetic word for me. Could he tell me? Of course he could! So he repeated, almost word for

Lowell and me, 2001

word, what the ladies in Texas had prophesied. I marveled, tucked it away in my heart, and waited on the Lord to bring it to pass.

PRAYERS FOR ADRIAN

Not only were there opportunities to share the love of Jesus with my patients, but also with my co-workers. Occasionally they would come to my office asking for prayer for family situations or problems.

One such visit, I vividly recall, was from my dear friend, Janelle. She requested prayer for her 12-year-old grandson, Adrian. He had been at a friend's house, and the two boys decided to build a bonfire. To get the fire going really well, they poured gasoline on it. The flames ignited, flying up onto Adrian's hand, arm, abdomen and legs. The doctor told them that he had third degree burns on 35-40 percent of his body. He had already been in the hospital burn unit for many days, and they were having difficulty getting a skin graft to adhere so the healing process could take place. Janelle wanted prayer that it would adhere on the next attempt.

The next morning as I rose up early for prayer, the Lord impressed upon me to use my prayer shawl while interceding, which I don't normally do. As I prayed in the Spirit, covering Adrian in prayer, God instructed me to get a prayer blanket for him. I thought, "I'll get a red one to symbolize the blood of Jesus." Immediately, I was corrected with God saying it was to be blue. I then saw, in my mind's eye, the blue fleece blanket that was to be used—it was upstairs. In many cultures, blue means peace, loyalty, faith, trust and wisdom. I thought I'd take it to my pastors and ask them to anoint it with oil and pray over it. Again, God had other plans. I was instructed to take it to another church, one I knew of but did not attend. I was to have those pastors anoint it with oil and pray over it. I was also instructed to get a Christmas card, including a specific amount of money to be placed inside. Adrian was to sign the card and give it to his mom. I was obedient to accomplish every detail. Then I delivered the card and ministered the love of God to Adrian and his mother. Adrian was deeply touched; he had desired to give his mom a gift but had no means to do so. He signed the card, thrilled to give it to his mom, along with the cash.

I shared lots of truth with Adrian, telling him how much the Father loved him and that God had many plans for him. He was scheduled for surgery that day, so he kept the anointed blanket close. The graft adhered and healing came. Thank you, Jesus!

Adrian's journey is not over. He is 16 now and still growing and learning. He's had some hard knocks recently, but I believe God's hand is upon him still, drawing Adrian into His kingdom.

Waiting for my flight to Uganda

AFRICAN ADVENTURES

In 2013, when I was sixty years old, God opened up new doors for me. It was announced at our church, that a group from California was preparing for an 18-day medical missions trip to Sri Lanka.

When we left church that day, Lowell informed me that I was supposed to go on that trip. "God didn't tell *me* that," I responded.

Lowell replied, "He didn't have to. He told me because He knew you'd have to ask me anyway."

God chose to speak to my husband first, because He knew Lowell would be hesitant to let me go. I contacted the organization and then sent in my application. I was soon notified that plans had changed. The authorities would not allow us to go to Sri Lanka, so the location had been changed to Uganda.

During my days of preparation, many people warned me not to go—it could be dangerous, and I may never return. But I was at peace, knowing that my steps were ordered by the Lord. And because He had called me on this mission trip, He would be with me every step of the way. One of the trip requirements was getting all of the vaccinations needed at my local health department to protect me from illnesses.

Before I knew it, I was on my way. I had never traveled outside of the United States before, and I didn't know one other person on the team.

In Uganda we spent our days traveling to various villages, setting up and tearing down our clinics, as we moved from one village to the next. We also traveled back into the bush on one occasion, where the community had never seen white people or a medical person.

In each village, our clinic was housed in the local church, which was one huge, open room—nothing fancy. We would set up different "stations" inside the church, using folding tables in each area to hold our supplies, and 10-15 white plastic chairs nearby for the patients. I soon discovered that those chairs

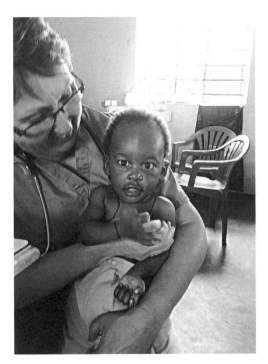

Checking a child's temperature
at a church medical clinic in
Uganda

were constantly full. As soon as a seat was vacated, it was filled with a new patient.

Each day, hundreds of people walked for miles to get to our clinics. They began lining up very early each morning. The line was always longer than the number of patients we'd be able to see in any given day. Many of them would camp overnight the night before the clinic opened, making a small fire and eating the meager meal they had brought with them. If they didn't make it into the clinic the first day, they would make camp again and stand in line the following morning. We treated over 6,000 people in 16 days.

Children from Kampala, Uganda
church orphanage and school
with my friend, Eddie

As we ushered the people into the clinic, they were triaged—their ailments or wounds were assessed, their treatment was decided, and they were assigned to the station that best met their need. A nurse was assigned to each station, and two doctors came along on the trip to oversee the nurses. A pharmacy was also set up at each clinic. Because the Africans spoke Swahili, a native interpreter was assigned to each station.

At the very first church clinic, as each patient visit was ending, I would ask through the interpreter if I could pray for them. While some said yes, most declined. When I did pray, it seemed to me that I just kept repeating the same prayer in English over and over again. The whole experience was like an assembly line, seeing a continuous stream of people, one after another, hour after hour.

After clinic, late that evening, God spoke to my heart clearly: "Do not ask them if you can pray for them. Tell them I sent you to Uganda to pray for them, will you receive prayer or not? Furthermore, you carry an anointing and authority because I sent you. You are not there for a vacation or trip but have been sent there to minister to my people. Also, do not pray in English but pray in your prayer language. They can't understand you anyway, and that's my perfect prayer for them."

The next day, I did as God instructed. I first told the interpreter exactly what to say to each patient: "God has sent me to Uganda to pray for you. Will you receive prayer or not?" She seemed more than a little surprised. As she began telling this to the patients, every person wanted prayer! At one point, I noticed that I was the only one praying over the patients. But I was not intimidated, because I knew in my heart that this was the very reason God had led me to Uganda.

Most of the churches we worked in housed orphanages. At the close of clinic the next evening, I saw a group of about ten orphans, eight to ten years old, playing and watching me. I asked them, "What do you want?" They said they wanted me to pray for them. There were nine boys and one girl waiting for my answer.

I told them to form a circle, holding hands, and then I would pray over them. I was planning to

pray one prayer over the group, but then I felt a
strong directive from the Spirit to pray for each one
individually. So I laid hands on each one, praying in
the spirit and prophesying. To each boy: "I call you
a mighty warrior for the Lord Jesus Christ." To the
little girl: "I call you a handmaiden of the Lord, and
you shall lead many to the Kingdom of God."

I was surprised to see what happened next. They
all began to dance, singing and shouting, "We are
mighty warriors for the Lord Jesus!" And the little

Children in a church orphanage
in Uganda

girl yelled out that she was a handmaiden of the Lord. The celebration soon attracted the attention of the adults, and everyone rejoiced.

(Several months later at home, during my early morning prayer, the Lord spoke to my heart, "Pray for My mighty warriors and My handmaiden today." I knew instantly who He was speaking about.)

One day we arrived with our clinic at yet another church. Just as I stepped out of the van, the locals ran to surround our bus, dancing, singing, and rejoicing because we were there. I looked down the road and saw a multitude of people coming. As far as the eye could see, I saw dark-skinned people arriving to be ministered to—spirit, soul, and body. In that moment, I realized that the prophecy spoken over me in Texas and Illinois was being fulfilled right before me. I looked up to heaven with a great big smile and prayed for them.

We worked 16 hours a day for 16 days. After the first week, our whole staff was getting tired.

The Lord woke me up one night, "You must guard your heart; many are becoming weary in well-doing, and the second week will be harder than the first. Some will begin to whine and complain, backbite and gossip. You must not give ear to it, or you will lose the anointing I have placed upon you."

Heeding His warning, I became very cautious. I began listening to praise and worship music with ear buds whenever I could. Soon I saw what God was talking about.

In the days ahead, as word traveled that a medical team had come, more and more Africans sought us out. One day, the interpreter told me that the patient seated before me was a pastor from deep in the bush. While in prayer that morning, God had instructed him to come many miles for the anointing. He was not ill, and he needed nothing else. He simply wanted me to lay hands on him and pray for the anointing. I was amazed, but I quickly recovered, recalling what God had told me before leaving home—that He would send people to me and that it was not about me, but it was all about Him. I knew this was the manifestation of what He had spoken.

This actually happened on three different days with three different pastors. Each of them said that God had spoken to them and instructed them to find me. When they saw me, they knew within themselves that I was the one to pray for them. I marveled at God's goodness and His amazingly detailed guidance for His people. I told each of them, "You shall have the anointing."

On our very last day in Uganda, I was asked to give the devotional for the medical team. I shared my testimony about how God had redeemed my past and how I had come to be with them on this trip. I could tell that it touched many of them.

When I finished, one of the paramedics in our group came up, knelt down in front of me, and asked forgiveness. I was shocked, having no idea why he was asking for my forgiveness. He confessed, "I have been rude to you and treated you poorly. I resented your coming, because you were new to our group."

I assured him that I truly hadn't noticed. He insisted that God had spoken to his heart, telling him that he needed to humble himself before me and ask me to forgive him. I did so immediately.

I had many wonderful experiences in Uganda. God answered numerous prayers and revealed His heart to me as well.

About a year later, I attended a women's conference with some women from our church. I greatly enjoyed

Joseph, a friend from Kampala, Uganda, who helps poor children and widows

Visiting a bush community with Pastor
Samuel's wife in Malawi

the conference and the fellowship. The next morning in
my hotel room, I knelt and prayed, "Father God, when
will I ever get to speak at a women's conference?"

He spoke to my heart loud and clear, "Africa is an
open door to you."

I was astonished and wondered what He meant. The
very next day, after returning home, Pastor Samuel
from Malawi, Africa, messaged me. He wrote that he
had been seeking God for a speaker for a women's

conference at his church, and he wanted me to come. He stated also that he had seen some pictures on Facebook of my trip to Uganda. I told him I would have to pray about it and talk to my husband.

At first, Lowell was very hesitant. This was not with a group. I would be going alone. Besides that, I had never met this pastor, and we had no mutual acquaintances.

I requested prayer about this matter from Dana, a homecare patient of mine at the time. Whenever I visited Dana for her medical assessment, I would always read a blessing to her when we were done. One day, I opened my blessing book and began reading to her. This time, I sensed something was different. I knew in my heart that this blessing was for me and not for Dana. I chose not to say anything and continued reading. When I finished, she said, "That is not my blessing; it is your blessing, and you are going to Malawi, Africa." We both knew God had spoken.

Upon arriving home, I asked Lowell to read the same blessing over me. At the end, he looked at me, "Yes, now I know you are to go to Malawi."

This was a big leap of faith for me, but I had no doubt that God was with me. I made preparations, and once again I was off to Africa. But this time I was traveling alone the entire trip.

Pastor Samuel and his family met me at the airport, welcoming me to Malawi. To my great surprise, I soon discovered that I was not one of many speakers for the upcoming conference; I was their only speaker. I was not to share for just one day during the week-long conference; I was to share every day! While I had spoken at women's meetings previously, I had never spoken at multiple services through an entire week, using an interpreter. I had no cell phone service to call my husband, but I knew he was covering me in prayer, along with several friends back home.

At the guest house, where I was staying, I spent much time in earnest prayer each day. What I had prepared to share would scarcely have covered the first day, much less the entire week.

God, as always, was faithful, giving me messages to share at every service with His beloved daughters. About 30 people attended the conference, mostly women, with a few men sitting in the back.

I was amazed at how far some of the women had traveled to get there, walking many miles or riding on the back of a pickup truck. They slept at the church, along with their children, lying on mats placed all over the cement floor. I was amazed! (American women would never do that.) One woman shared with me that she had sold her goat in order to have the money to come.

We had wonderful services. Their praise and worship was delightfully vibrant and free. We danced and praised God. They complimented me: "You dance like an African woman." I reminded them that *"to the weak I became as weak, that I might win the weak. I have become all things to all men, that I might by all means save some"* (I Corinthians 9:22). "When I'm with the Africans I do as they do, when I'm with the Amish, I do as the Amish do, and when I'm with our Hispanic friends, I do as they do—all to the glory of God. "

Stirring a pot of corn meal (seama)
for the Malawi women's conference lunch

While in Malawi, I got to attend a funeral service. I was also privileged to visit some native homes, which were simple grass huts with dirt floors.

A couple years later, Pastor Samuel had an opportunity to come to the States. He stayed in our home for a few days, and I took him to meet Dana. She could not go to Africa, but Africa came to her. Pastor Samuel prayed over her and was a great encouragement, both to her and to me.

We also hosted a gathering in our home so that our friends and family could meet Pastor Samuel. I was pleased that we were able to bless his church with a financial gift as well.

With Omar and Cruz, daughter Aleida, and son Michael at church New Years Eve party

BLESSED OF THE LORD

TO WHOM MUCH IS GIVEN, MUCH IS REQUIRED.

In 2013, Lowell and I purchased a repossessed farmhouse, one-half mile down the road from our house. Our plan was to fix it up and rent it. Hispanic friends from our church, Omar and Cruz, contacted us about living there and helping us restore it. Their desire was to live in the country, closer to the church, and for their children to attend a smaller school, away from the city. We said that would be fine. So they moved in with their three children, two teenage boys and a younger daughter, about the time school was starting in late summer.

They began with the barns, painting and making repairs. Our plans for the house were to install new siding and windows, along with insulation, before winter.

I purchased fire and smoke alarms and asked Omar to install them. The next time I visited the

After the fire: the old farmhouse where Omar and Cruz and their family were living

farmhouse, they were still sitting on the table. With a sense of great urgency, I stressed to him that the alarms must be up and working quickly, or they couldn't live there. It was an old house that Lowell planned to rewire, but he hadn't begun that job yet.

It was late October, early in the morning, when one of Omar's boys was awakened by a smoke alarm going off. He got up to check it out and discovered that the house was on fire! He quickly roused the rest of the family. They all rushed outside and then called us. We hurried to the farm, calling the fire department on the way. The house was in flames! We lost the garage and the back side of the house. Fortunately, we had not yet replaced the windows or siding on the back of the house, but part of the new roof had been utterly destroyed.

As the firemen worked to extinguish the fire, I went into warrior mode, marching around that house, declaring and decreeing that the enemy had been caught stealing from us and destroying our property. I commanded, in agreement with the Word of God, that he had to pay us back seven times what he had taken—see John 10:10 and Proverbs 6:30-31.

(My prayers were not answered immediately, but years later, Ben bought the house with a loan from us, and he completely restored it. The same appraiser before the fire and after the restoration marveled at the beautiful transformation. Its value had increased four times.)

As family and friends arrived, we cried and prayed for each other, thanking God that everyone was safe. However, our dear friends lost everything they owned and had no renter's insurance to replace anything. Omar laid his head on Lowell's shoulder, weeping, and Lowell wrapped his arms around him in an effort to comfort him. The news of the fire spread rapidly, and church friends and family members gathered at the scene to offer support and help in any way they could.

Since it was early morning, we invited the whole crowd, approximately 30, to our home for a breakfast

Omar, Cruz, and family in our home,
enjoying food and fellowship

of pancakes, bacon, and eggs. As we began eating in shifts, I sent Ben on a quick trip to the grocery store for more food. All of the women pitched in and helped with the meal preparation and cleanup. Then our meal together turned into a church service, a time of fellowship and praising God.

We invited Omar's family to move in with us. It was no hardship because we had plenty of rooms and beds. We believed God had given us an opportunity to love this family. They taught us a lot, and we learned to eat authentic Mexican food and loved it!

Our friends were a huge blessing during the time they lived with us in our log home. Omar and his boys insulated our garage and helped cut firewood for the winter months ahead. We shared our faith experiences and encouraged each other.

One Sunday, a man from our church asked me, "Is it true the Mexicans are living with you?"

I responded, "Yes."

He questioned, "Why would you let Mexicans live with you?"

Appalled, I answered, "To show you what love looks like, because apparently you don't know!"

That January, Lowell and I traveled to Florida on a business trip. Omar, Cruz and their children, along with our Ben, stayed home. While we were gone, our area at home was hit by a snowstorm that left some people stranded at church. Lowell and I were in our hotel room when Cruz called to ask if her sister and children could join them in our home for a few days. Their car had gotten stuck in a snowdrift.

I said, "Of course! There is plenty of room in our house; bring them home." There were now 11 people living at our house and using our car.

After hanging up, the devil came to tempt Lowell and cause him to stumble. My husband asked me, "How come I'm feeling a little used?" I informed him it was the enemy, trying to stir up trouble. Lowell said he was going down the hall to fill our ice bucket, and I had better pray, because he wanted a word from God about this when he got back.

I assured him that I would pray. I received an answer as soon as I began praying. The Lord reminded me that *"The one to whom much is given, much is required" (Luke 12:48)*.

When Lowell came back into the room, he looked at me and said, "Well...?"

I quoted the scripture God had given me and asked, "Are we blessed or not?" He began to cry, and we got down on our knees, repented, and asked forgiveness. Peace flooded our spirits, and we knew God had spoken.

It wasn't long before our houseguests became like family. We sensed the leading of the Lord to help them get back on their feet again, so we gave them ten percent of the insurance money we'd received for the house fire. After moving to their own place, we remained close friends for many years.

Five years later, at 42 years of age, our dear Cruz was diagnosed with cancer. After they shared the news with us, I was deeply grieved. Going directly to her side, I prayed for her healing and restoration. Lowell and I rallied around the family with love and support. Cruz's mother and sisters became her caregivers. Again, they showed us how family should be, tenderly loving and supporting one another.

As Cruz's extended family gathered each evening to love and support her, they also grieved together, because she was not improving. Although Cruz was dying, she ministered to each of her loved ones, and they often celebrated communion together as a family. She desired that each one would continue serving God and not give up on their faith. During her short time on earth, she had led many to Jesus.

One evening, she called me aside to be alone with her. She thanked me for the many ways I had truly loved her, that she would never forget me, and that she returned my love. I held her in my arms for 45 minutes, praying in the Spirit. During that prayer, I released her, letting her go. She died peacefully the next day with her family at her bedside.

My dear friend, Cruz

Cruz was like a sister to me, and the love we shared went deep. In my heart I see Cruz dancing before the throne of grace, praising God and worshiping. I know she's doing what she loved most—praising God. Even in her dying, she glorified God. I am eternally grateful for the opportunity I had to know and love Cruz and her family.

Lowell and I sold our Red Honda Gold Wing motorcycle and purchased this Honda Gold Wing trike.

THE LOST PHONE

For several years, Lowell and I owned a red Honda Gold Wing motorcycle. About ten years ago, we decided we'd ride it all the way to Pennsylvania to see his cousins, Danny and Edna. We had such a marvelous time of fellowship with them, and we thoroughly enjoyed our visit. Before we left for home, they wanted to take pictures of us with our motorcycle. I was holding my cell phone, but not wanting it in the pictures, had laid it down. After our photo shoot, we jumped onto the cycle, and away we went. Our destination was a graduation party two hours away for a nephew. We were looking forward to seeing more family there.

As we left Danny and Edna's driveway, we encountered road construction. Lowell hit a bump fairly hard, jolting me, but we rode on. We arrived at the party and visited with family. Deciding to take some pictures to share with Ben, I looked for my phone but couldn't find it. I looked everywhere, including the bike trunk and the bag on the back of the carrier. I asked Lowell if he had seen it. He hadn't.

Where did I have it last? Oh yes, it was when we took pictures with Danny and Edna! I probably laid it on top of our bag, which was strapped to the cycle, and it had fallen off when we hit that large bump. Lowell and I prayed together for the phone to be found. It held all my work contact information.

Amazingly, just the week before, God had prompted me to put a security lock on my phone, which I did, though I had never done so before. Lowell also called Danny and Edna, who looked for it without success. They even searched the road construction site. I continued to pray, thanking God in advance for bringing it back to me.

I convinced Lowell to travel the two hours back to Danny and Edna's. Because my phone had a bright pink OtterBox cover, I was quite certain I would be able to spot it. We retraced our route with my eyes constantly scanning the road. No phone. Arriving back at Danny and Edna's, Lowell and I drove up and down the road. Still no phone.

We examined the pictures in Edna's camera to see if the phone's location was visible there. It was not on the bag strapped to the carrier. It was under the carrier. Lowell said that could make a huge difference as to where it fell off, possibly an hour down the road. We spent the night, got up the next morning, and prepared to leave. I continued to pray, trusting God to help me find it.

Lowell stated his conclusion. "Just give up. You know you won't find it."

That upset me, and I asked, "Does Father God know where it is?"

"Of course he does," he responded.

"Then He can tell me where it is."

My heart felt heavy as we headed out once again. I wanted to cry, but I didn't. About two miles down the road, I happened to look ahead. There it was in the middle of the road—my phone! As Lowell slowed down, I jumped off and ran to pick it up. The cover was missing, and the screen was cracked, but it still turned on. Thank you, Jesus! Looking around, I spotted my OtterBox cover a little further back in some weeds at the side of the road. I knew that someone had found it and tried to tamper with it. I guessed that they had removed the cover and tossed it out of their car window. Then when they couldn't open my phone, due to the security lock, they tossed that next. I called Edna and Danny to tell them the good news. They were shocked that I had even found it.

Because I had insurance coverage on my phone, I took it to the cell phone dealer the next day, explaining what had happened. The bad news was that they couldn't replace my phone, due to its age. The good news was that they gave me an upgraded phone!

Next I contacted the OtterBox company, telling them my story as well. They confirmed that the OtterBox could not have fallen off, but it would have been intentionally removed. Because I had owned the cover for more than one year, they said they wouldn't normally replace it. However, the gentleman I had spoken to loved my story so much that he decided to give me a new one with my choice of color.

Praise God! I had found favor with God and man. I did my happy dance after that phone call, and then I shared my story with everyone I saw for the next several days.

Lowell and I, married 50 years

50TH ANNIVERSARY

On November 21, 2020, Lowell and I celebrated a very important milestone in our lives—fifty years of marriage! I consider that achievement nothing less than a mighty miracle of God. Very few couples on my side of the family have ever come close to celebrating 50 years together. My parents were married multiple times and set a very poor example.

Our marriage has not been flawless. Because we married young, at 17 and 19 years of age, we had a lot of growing up to do—a lot to learn. There was much to work through as we matured, especially in those early years. We are truly grateful for the married couples God brought into our lives who mentored us as newlyweds, as well as those who modeled what a godly marriage looks like.

Lowell and I had very humble beginnings, and we faced many difficult struggles, particularly in the first few years of marriage. Our first house was located in a back alley of Detroit. It was a tiny house—just 8 feet by 16 feet—and held everything we owned. The bathroom was so small it had no sink. There was barely room for the tub and toilet. We sat on the toilet to brush our teeth over the tub. In the main room of the house, we had a three-quarter size bed. When friends came to visit, it served as our sofa as well, where we sat to play card games and eat

Our current log home sits on 40 acres.

Our grandchildren (left to right): Ezra, Julia, Zachary, Sophia holding Elijah, Noah, William, and Carter

snacks. Even so, we made wonderful memories with those friends. Through the years (looking back), I have often said, "We lived off of love." And we did love each other, deeply.

We had made our vows before God and were committed, both to God and to each other, to make our union work and last. If we had a disagreement, we learned quickly that it was best to settle the matter and make up before the lights went out. I was not yet aware of the Scripture from Ephesians: *"'Be angry, and do not sin': do not let the sun go down on your wrath, nor give place to the devil"*

(Ephesians 4:26-27). We humbled ourselves often, asking forgiveness of each other.

From the beginning of our marriage, I have recognized Lowell as the head of our household. I did not want to imitate the destruction I saw my mother bring to her relationship with my father by her lack of respect and honor for him. However, I have always said that while Lowell was the head, I was the neck, and the head can't do much without the neck for support!

We worked at our marriage, and frankly, we still do. Good marriages don't just happen; they require continual tending and a giving of oneself to the other. We have also kept our passion burning and have enjoyed the physical aspect of our union

Our family, the fruit of our marriage covenant

throughout our 50 years. We delight in each other and are best friends.

You've heard the saying—The family that prays together, stays together. Lowell and I can give testimony to the truth of that statement. I do recall an extremely difficult time in our marriage. At one point, we got down on our knees, repented, asked and received forgiveness from each other, and asked God to restore our marriage. That was almost 20 years ago, and we are still going strong. Praise God!

We know without a doubt that our Source is Father God. From Him we have been given strength, steadfastness in our relationship, and oh-so-many blessings! Yes, we have messed up and made mistakes, but forgiveness cleans the slate every time! I am happy to share that we have not simply endured fifty years together, but we have weathered the storms of life and celebrated the blessings of God, together, with thankful hearts.

My love for Lowell now is greater and deeper than the day I said, "I do." And I know he says the same of me. We take joy in the love that God placed in our hearts for each other all those years ago, and we have watched it grow beyond our wildest dreams. *"May the Lord make your love increase and overflow for each other..." (1 Thessalonians 3:12a NIV)*. God certainly has done that, and our cup overflows!

Author

CONCLUSION

Father God has promised me that my latter days would be far greater than my former days. I have been blessed coming in and going out. It's been a growing process, and it still is.

While there have been many struggles and heartaches, God has made me an overcomer, delivering me from the yoke of bondage. He also destroyed the generational curse over me, setting me free from all of it.

I have eyes to see and ears to hear Him speak to my heart. I have His Spirit living and abiding on the inside of me. By the Word of God that is alive in me, He leads me and guides me. *"You are of God, little children, and have overcome them, because He who is in you is greater than he who is in the world. . ."* (1 John 4:4). *"For there is no partiality with God"* (Romans 2:11). What God has done for me, He can do for you. *"Come near to God and he will come near to you..."* (James 4:8 NIV).

It has been said that we cannot change our past, and we cannot change the fact that people will act, or have acted, in certain ways towards us. We cannot change the inevitable. Only God can change the hearts of mankind. Life is 10% what happens to us, and 90% how we react to it. We must live with the choices we make. *"Do not be deceived: God cannot be mocked. A man reaps what he sows"* (Galatians 6:7 NIV).

My heart has been fixed on trusting in the Lord most of my life. While I was able to forgive the abuse, God has never let me forget where I came from—my roots. I believe those memories serve to keep me humble and give me a very thankful heart. I recognize it's only because of Jesus that I am abundantly blessed today.

"When we walk with the wise we shall become wise, for a companion of fools will be destroyed" (Proverbs 13:20).

"So I will restore to you the years that the swarming locust has eaten, The crawling locust, The consuming locust, And the chewing locust, My great army which I sent among you. You shall eat in plenty and be satisfied, And praise the name of the Lord your God, Who has dealt wondrously with you; And My people

shall never be put to shame. Then you shall know that I am in the midst of Israel: I am the Lord your God And there is no other. My people shall never be put to shame. And it shall come to pass afterward That I will pour out My Spirit on all flesh; Your sons and your daughters shall prophesy, Your old men shall dream dreams, Your young men shall see visions. And also on My menservants and on My maidservants I will pour out My Spirit in those days" (Joel 2:25-29.)

The truth is, God can bring purpose to even the negative things we have endured. God doesn't waste anything, including life's harshest experiences. If we have a willing heart, He will use them to form us into the people He desires us to be. As I opened myself up to Him, God built on my experiences for His purposes and for my inner healing. Out of my past, God poured into me forgiveness, mercy, and compassion. He has orchestrated my life to minister these very graces to hurting people, everywhere I go. Never having forgotten where I came from, I marvel how far He has taken me. Though short in stature, God certainly did make me big on the inside.

To God be all honor and glory!

The author may be contacted
by email at lgraber1953@gmail.com